THE SYNTHETIC EYE |

"Photograph of Abraham Lincoln
taking a selfie."

Fred Ritchin

THE SYNTHETIC EYE |

Photography Transformed
in the Age of AI

To those who continue the search for a better way.

"Silent circuits hum,
Machines learn
and grow stronger,
Human fate unsure."

A haiku generated by Sia Kordestani and ChatGPT[1]

"Adam and Eve and the apple of knowledge,"
inspired by the work of Werner Heisenberg.

Preface

In 1982, at the dawn of the digital image revolution, *National Geographic* used a computer to modify a horizontal photograph of the pyramids of Giza so that it would better fit on its vertical cover, shifting one pyramid closer and partially behind the other. Two years later I interviewed the magazine's editor, who defended the alteration, viewing it not as a falsification but, as I wrote then in the *New York Times Magazine*, "merely the establishment of a new point of view, as if the photographer had been retroactively moved a few feet to one side."[2] I was astonished. It seemed to me that *National Geographic* had just introduced to photography a concept from science fiction – virtual time travel – as if one could revisit a scene and photograph it again.

Concerned by the emergence of this software's ability to quickly and undetectably modify a photograph, I suggested in the article that "in the not-too-distant future, realistic-looking images will probably have to be labeled, like words, as either fiction or nonfiction, because it may be impossible to tell them apart. We may have to rely on the image maker, and not the image, to tell us into which category certain pictures fall."

Now, forty years later, not only has image modification software been made widely accessible and often *de rigueur* for photographers, but the medium itself has been effectively simulated. Artificial intelligence systems have emerged that can generate photorealistic images of events that never occurred and people who never existed, without the use of a camera. The result is that the photograph's evidentiary, dialectical relationship with the visible and the real has been largely displaced by manipulated and synthetic imagery of the world as one wants it to be.

Many of the billions of synthetic images now being generated are uploaded to join the mass of imagery already in existence (one recent survey concluded that almost 200 million photos are made each hour), much of it manipulated, undermining the clarity and certitude of the actual photographs that they so closely resemble. Meanwhile, we are only just beginning to reckon with the potential of image generators to transcend the photorealistic and provoke a rethinking of the world in more nuanced, expansive ways.

Photography was quite different in the 20th-century age of film. It could be magical to watch an image slowly emerge onto a white piece of paper as it floated in a chemical bath. As one stood alone in a darkened room, it could have seemed as if there were spirits resurrecting people and scenes from a receding past, alchemy keeping them from slipping away. While absolute truths were elusive, it was revelation enough to be able to summon up a sense of what might have happened or of who had once been.

There might also be a humility in not knowing; maybe the camera recorded something the photographer might not have sufficiently registered or even seen, unsure of what image would emerge until the film was processed and the print was made. If one remained in a meditative state of mind, the act of photographing could resemble holding a net, hoping for the butterflies to arrive, and then finding other valuable, unexpected treasures that had somehow managed to insert themselves and be rendered visible.

Photography could be a way of immersing oneself in life, not separating from it. Henri Cartier-Bresson, who once characterized photojournalism for me as "keeping a journal with a camera," defined photography as "not documentary, but intuition, a poetic experience. It's drowning yourself, dissolving yourself, and then sniff, sniff, sniff – being sensitive to coincidence. You can't go looking for it; you can't want it, or you won't get it. First you must lose your self. Then it happens."[3] The Mexican photographer Graciela Iturbide described it in similar terms. "When I'm taking pictures, I even forget that I have a camera. When I shoot I forget about everything. Light comes, death comes, people go in and out in costume – and it's like a play."[4] The resulting images could resonate with the world from which they came, reflecting its deeper currents while recording that which existed even if for only a fractional second, but enough for a future viewer to share in the experience knowing that, at some level, it had occurred.

In our digital environment, cameras and cellphones (over 90% of photographs are now made on cellphones) allow an instant review of our images. Photographers no longer have to wait for film to be processed and printed, wondering if what they think they saw has been recorded; the evidence is available immediately on the camera itself. Perceptions and preconceptions can be confirmed; a less-than-idealized image can be viewed as only a draft to be molded, assisted by a plethora of editing software. Self-portraits, introspective explorations produced with the evidence gathered from the lens, have in recent years morphed into "selfies," images to be uploaded and immediately shared as a way of demonstrating the excitement of our lives to others, as well as to ourselves.

Rather than the recording of a confrontation with the visible, photography has evolved into a medium that is increasingly designed to please, with software inside the camera to enhance the image even before it emerges, and other software to remedy its perceived failings after it has been produced. People can be made to look thinner and more fit, their skin toned and their wrinkles removed; their expression in one image can be placed into another; an out-of-focus photograph can be sharpened. The nuances of light that are essential to photography (originally meaning "writing or drawing with light") are filtered and homogenized, algorithms determining how they should look. When smoke from wildfires across the United States turned the skies strangely orange, for example, cellphone cameras were incapable of acknowledging the transformation and showed them as gray ("Your Phone Wasn't Built for the Apocalypse," as an article in the *Atlantic* put it[5]).

In this new paradigm, photography becomes increasingly an expression of consumer entitlement. While the consumers in a capitalist society have always been told they are right, now the prosumers, the individuals who both produce many of the nearly 2 trillion photographs made annually and consume them, are also thought to deserve a customized version of the real. While it appears to have been photographed, the world around us instead has been largely reconfigured to please.

As computational photography emerged over recent decades to subvert the evidence of the lens, generative artificial intelligence systems have done away with the need for a camera altogether. After training on an archive of billions of images online, software can now produce images in response to text prompts that imitate the look of actual photographs. Many of the images that result can be problematic, both racist and misogynistic, utilizing visual tropes that are offensive in large part because of the archival content on which they were trained. But the process can also be a revelation, evoking a sense of discovery not unlike that which might have been felt, and some might still feel, while waiting for a photographic image to emerge in the darkroom.

Unlike image modification software, which allows users to alter photographs in specific ways to match their desires, the images generated via artificial intelligence can be impossible to predict, sometimes interesting but also often disappointing. Provoking such a system into generating an image that is as enlightening as it is unexpected can be difficult, not unlike trying to communicate with a foreigner who speaks a different language, or may speak no language at all. The back-and-forth of it is somewhat like the "exquisite corpse," the Surrealist game in which each player imagines and draws a section of a person's body, adding to the parts that others have already drawn without being able to see them until the very end.

These algorithms are unpredictable even to those who created them, many of their preferences unknown. Asking them to conjure people, scenes, and events that may never have existed, or to depict them from the differing perspectives of, say, a poet or a hawk, requires the imagining of possibilities rather than being confined to previous perceptions of reality. The image that results, while looking like a realistic photograph, may also be a wolf in sheep's clothing, a puzzle asking for further reflection from a source whose merits are not at all clear.

Defining parameters too specifically can, however, lead to uninspired responses, as if the system is attempting to please by imitating the simplistic, conventional images that are rampant online. The most productive text prompts, in my experience, open up a creative space in which the image generator responds not to a command but to a series of suggestions, hints, and possibilities, engaged in an open-ended dialogue as a collaborator seemingly capable of autonomous input, rather than being subservient to the explicit wishes of the client.

There can be something indeterminate and tantalizing about this process, signifying what might be rather than confirming what already is. For example, when I asked one image generator, DreamStudio, to respond to the prompt, "Adam and Eve and the apple of knowledge" with the work of Werner Heisenberg as inspiration, I was requesting that it reimagine a fundamental origin story according to the worldview of a quantum physicist who articulated "the uncertainty principle." Rather than reflecting the Bible's Newtonian tale of cause and effect that cast Adam and Eve as central players in a morality tale, evicted from Paradise after having eaten the forbidden apple and then transformed into husband and wife, I was curious to explore another, looser rendition, even as I asked that the image appear as if made on "analog film."

How to interpret the image? Is Eve depicted nude while Adam is clothed, the apple hovering between them, because she was the first to eat the apple and understand, as it says in Genesis: "for God knows that on the day you eat thereof, your eyes shall be opened, and you shall be as gods, knowing good and evil"?[6] Is she asking him to eat from the tree to confirm the

Biblical assertion, "the eyes of both of them were opened, and they knew that they were naked"? Or is the apple made to hover there because, unlike in the Bible story where Eve makes him eat the apple, she is acknowledging his free will, and offering him the choice as to whether he wants to join her? Or, perhaps, might this image be just another manifestation of misogyny, the woman shown unclothed, as the generator regurgitates the stereotypes upon which it was trained?

Did the artificial intelligence actually comprehend that my prompt was asking for Heisenberg's perspective as a quantum physicist? Is that why the apple appears to float when Isaac Newton's law of gravitation used the example of an apple to explain why it would in fact fall straight down? Is the floating apple meant to reflect Heisenberg's perspective of uncertainty as a counterpoint to Newton's law? Or is there something richer going on here, with the presence of the apple of knowledge?

If we could take a bite ourselves, might it lead us into a myriad of possibilities, reminiscent of Jorge Luis Borges's mystical short story "The Aleph," first published in 1945, which describes an encounter with something that is little more than an inch in diameter but in which not only "all space was there, actual and undiminished," but "each thing...was infinite things"?[7] Should I have made Borges, a master of non-linearity, into a kind of "meta-photographer" as well?

It's clear that image generators can do much more than simulate photographs, and as artificial intelligence matures they are sure to substantially expand their range. As Marshall McLuhan pointed out, in the short term the content of every new medium resembles a previous one. In the 19th century, for example, Pictorialist photography borrowed from the look of painting; in the early days of cinema the movies that were produced tended to look theatrical; at first, "digital photography" resembled the analog kind. But in the long term, media evolve, the paradigm shifts, and they grow into much richer versions of themselves.

For the moment, the photorealistic possibilities of artificial intelligence systems like DALL·E, Midjourney, Adobe Firefly, and Stability Diffusion have captivated society's imagination while terrifying observers with their ability to create false narratives that subvert the credibility attributed to photographs (similar discussions have emerged concerning text generated by AI). Meanwhile, deepfakes, utilizing photographs, video and sound that already exist, are being produced to show people seeming to say and do things that they never did: government leaders hatching plots, a high school principal spouting racism, and women, many of them celebrities, placed in pornographic scenes.

Democracies are destabilized by the widespread introduction of such fabrications, which also taint, sometimes fatally, the evidence of actual photographs and videos. How can one feel empowered as a citizen when differentiating among these various kinds of media begins to seem hopeless, or so time-consuming as to be out of one's reach? Our perceptions of collective and personal histories can be amplified but also undermined, at times maliciously, by the ease with which imagery can be produced to support nearly any point of view. These images, once uploaded, may be used to train future image generators that further uproot us from the world that we had previously inhabited.

However, these systems can also be used to provoke a re-thinking of the world that challenges pieties, rebukes colonialist assertions, and embraces perspectives reflecting the incalculable diversity of humans as well as other life forms. While photography, for example, is unable to depict the future or distant path, or to access our thoughts and dreams, these arenas are relatively easy to explore via synthetic imagery generated by text prompts, sometimes in useful and practical ways.

For the moment, unable to differentiate the images that record what existed from those that show what never happened, we find ourselves in search of another compass. French critic Roland Barthes's landmark assertion, "One day, quite some

time ago, I happened on a photograph of Napoleon's youngest
brother, Jerome, taken in 1852. And I realized then, with an
amazement I have not been able to lessen since: 'I am looking
at eyes that looked at the Emperor,'"[8] has become considerably
less operative. It is already possible to view historical figures in
a multitude of ways and, with little effort, to make the image
appear to be photographic. Unlike that moment in 1980 when
Barthes signaled his amazement, photographs in the age of
artificial intelligence can come to seem comparatively dry and
unimaginative, limited by their attachment to only one version
of the real.

What then has photography become? Can it be revitalized and
made to communicate with more authenticity, its credibility as
a witness restored? Can photographers, in part as a response to
the emergence of the synthetic and the photorealistic, expand
their visions while embracing new strategies of production and
presentation? Should we define a "nonfiction photography"
that excludes synthetic and highly manipulated images, and
make it clear to the reader where the boundaries lie? And can
artificial intelligence be engaged with in ways that allow it to
extend productively and responsibly into new arenas, including
those beyond photography's reach?

These are a few of the questions that humans, as well as the
institutions that are meant to serve and represent them, will have
to respond to as thoughtfully as possible in the very near future.
The Synthetic Eye is meant to help provoke and, if possible,
accelerate such a discussion, cognizant that it is less the future
of photography that is at issue than that of the larger world.

Chapter One

Exiting the Photographic Universe

"At the Whitney Museum, New York City."
Cellphone image by the author, August 2023.

"Having exhausted every possibility, at the moment when he was coming full circle Antonino realized that photographing photographs was the only course that he had left – or, rather, the true course that he had obscurely been seeking all this time."

Italo Calvino, "The Adventure of a Photographer," 1955

In his short story "The Adventure of a Photographer"[1] published nearly 70 years ago, Italo Calvino presciently described our obsessively photographed world from deep within the analog era of film. Almost half a century before the advent of today's omnipresent camera phones, he writes of droves of city dwellers likened to hunters who, as the weather becomes warmer, go out on Sundays photographing one another before returning to anxiously await the arrival of the developed pictures.

These people's lives, the story suggests, are unfulfilled until the photographs are before them, their experiences remaining otherwise somewhat vague and abstract. Not until they receive the photographs do they appear "to take tangible possession of the day they spent," so it is only then that their views of a landscape, a playing child, even the light reflecting upon a spouse, are concretized and validated, no longer subject to the vagaries of memory.

Antonino, a non-photographer, is the protagonist of Calvino's story. He decides to join the others and, after meeting a woman, Bice, tries to capture her essence with his camera. Aware of the many ways in which he could photograph her, as well as those versions of her that he cannot extract with his camera, he seeks a strategy to combine the two. As a result, he decides to photograph her constantly, both day and night, intent on exhausting all possibilities.

It also exhausts her. Antonino photographs Bice nude and tells her, "I've got you now." She bursts into tears, bewildered, and soon leaves him. He falls into a serious depression and begins to keep a photographic diary in which, not leaving his home, he stares vacantly ahead while photographing her absence. Then Antonino looks at what he has done, lays out the imagery on newspapers and photographs the ensemble, juxtaposing public and private images in a way that resembles the chaotic mixture that populates the internet today. He concludes that perhaps a "true, total photography" consists of this private imagery being displayed "against the creased background of massacres and coronations."

Finally, increasingly frustrated, Antonino comes to an epiphany, understanding "that photographing photographs was the only course that he had left – or, rather, the true course he had obscurely been seeking all this time."

This, of course, is not that different from the way image generators work today: artificial intelligence systems train on an enormous archive of photographs, placed online along with their descriptions, to generate their own images based on those previously made. If the story were to be written today, Antonino could continue to generate new images, synthetic ones, resembling Bice, nude, clothed, young or old, making love with him or with someone else, or use previous photographs of her to generate deepfakes, placing her, without her consent, in tawdry situations where she never had been. Or Bice, should she want to take more control of her own image, might be making and distributing endless selfies with her cellphone while using software filters to enhance her look, a self-absorption that can be, just like Antonino's stalking, obsessive and ultimately unhealthy. As Monica Lewinsky, herself a longtime victim of online bullying, put it, "The whole point of a filter is saying: I want to look better, which means you're not good enough."[2]

Now the image can manifest in many more ways, some of them exceedingly destructive. The actress Scarlett Johansson, whose likeness has been utilized in pornographic deepfakes, forcefully characterized the situation: "The internet is a vast wormhole of darkness that eats itself."[3] (As of this writing, there are no federal laws in the United States protecting the victims of non-consensual deepfakes, many of whom are female celebrities.) Unlike in 1955, it can be much more difficult for images, no matter how nasty and victimizing, to be forgotten and erased.

"This person does not exist."

A synthetic image that simulates a photograph, produced by a GAN (generative adversarial network) on the website thispersondoesnotexist.com, February 2022.

"This person does not exist."

In his 1859 essay, "On Photography," the critic Charles Baudelaire disparaged the new medium just two decades after its invention, calling it no more than a recording device to be utilized by "the secretary and clerk of whoever needs an absolute factual exactitude in his profession... But if it be allowed to encroach upon the domain of the impalpable and the imaginary, upon anything whose value depends solely upon the addition of something of a man's soul, then it will be so much the worse for us!"[4]

Despite Baudelaire's protestations, photography came to be considered an artistic practice and, as a result, twenty-five years after his essay appeared, photographers were able to retain copyright of their own imagery in the United States. However, only a century later the "factual exactitude" that Baudelaire attributed to the medium, "enrich[ing] the tourist's album and restor[ing] to his eye the precision which his memory may lack," would no longer be taken for granted, an enormous transformation encouraged by the increased malleability of the digital environment. While the medium is now widely accepted as an art, exhibited in the most prestigious museums and galleries worldwide and with photographic prints being sold for high prices, its reputation as a reliable recording device has been profoundly undercut.

In the 1990s, as Photoshop became available to the public at a relatively affordable price, photographic alterations began to be reconceived as necessary enhancements rather than deceptive manipulations. Magazines started to regularly modify photographs, particularly on their covers. In 1994, *Time* magazine darkened and blurred a police department photograph of O. J. Simpson, who had been arrested on suspicion of having committed a double murder, and rationalized it to the magazine's readers the following week as merely an attempt to lift "a common police mug shot to the level of art, with no sacrifice to truth." That same year, the front page of *Newsday* featured a composite image of feuding Olympic ice skaters Nancy Kerrigan and Tonya Harding, who were shown to be

already skating together in an anticipated meeting that was
to take place the following day. "Tonya, Nancy to Meet at
Practice" was quite possibly the first "future news photograph"
ever published; superimposed at the bottom in smaller type,
an explanation described how the athletes were made to "appear
to skate together."

Since then, the modification of photographs has become
commonplace, the photograph itself considered more of a first
draft to be altered than an authoritative rendering of what was
in front of the lens. If "the medium is the message," as Marshall
McLuhan once put it, the message of photography today in
the digital environment is the malleability of the real, not its
recording as something fixed for future contemplation.

So, unlike Kodak's film-era advertisements, which promoted
photography as a way to "let the memories begin," the Google
Pixel camera now features itself as having both a Magic
Eraser and a Face Unblur, among many other functions, some
performed automatically within the camera, outside the
photographer's control. Google also offers a Portrait Light
software that allows the user to change the lighting of the
photograph *after* it is made, and its Magic Editor can be used
to "create new content to fill in the gaps after repositioning your
subject."[5] As a 2023 article in *PetaPixel* summed it up, "Google
Photos Will Let You Completely Change Your Pictures with AI."[6]
Formerly a recording of what was visible at a specific moment,
the photograph is now frequently relegated to the role of
a first impression to be "perfected" with digital technology.

If we can "completely change your pictures with AI," we can
completely change the world to match your preconceptions.
Rather than observing, this kind of computational photography
advances a form of proprietary looking in which what we want
to see is realized as a form of consumer entitlement, an eighth
day of creation with outcomes guided by camera manufacturers
and software developers. No longer a dialectical relationship

"The first photograph ever made."

with the world, the image is increasingly constructed according to consumerist fantasies of beauty and happiness, a map of desires allowed to supersede the realities that photographs previously explored. As Stephen Shankland described it for CNET, "With a sweep of my mouse, Photoshop could generate a nice patch of blue sky to replace an annoying dead tree branch cluttering my shot of luscious yellow autumn leaves. Smartphones are now making similar decisions on their own as you tap the shutter button."[7]

A recent Google television ad for its Pixel 8 phone, also available online, features a photograph in which a man is pictured tossing a baby up above him at the beach, and then immediately afterwards a finger is shown sliding along the cellphone's screen so that the baby is re-positioned much higher in the sky, dangerously so. "What's wrong with that?" a tech columnist for a major American newspaper asked me in a recent interview, suggesting that the image modification was innocuous. I responded that not only might the modified image, if uncaptioned and explained, call into question the reliability of a family album, but if anyone should attempt to similarly toss a baby inspired by the image that they had seen, the results could be catastrophic. On the other hand, perhaps such images will soon have minimal impact as people's skepticism rises.

Having absorbed these lessons, we humans make ourselves minor deities of a world that does not exist, while remaining powerless to effect substantive change in the actual world we inhabit, especially given how little we now may know about what is going on. Synthetic images that simulate photographs invoke so many convincing scenarios that the actual ones become no more real than any other, the "liar's dividend" making it harder to challenge those in power.

"A capitalist society requires a culture based on images. It needs to furnish vast amounts of entertainment to stimulate buying and anesthetize the injuries of class, race, and sex," Susan Sontag wrote in 1977, before the massive onslaught of imagery that proliferates today. "Social change is replaced by a change in images. The freedom to consume a plurality of images and goods is equated with freedom itself. The narrowing of free political choice to free economic consumption requires the unlimited production and consumption of images."[8]

Not long ago, a single photograph on the front page of a newspaper or magazine could focus society's attention. Now, while images have become the currency of the land, there are so many – one estimate put it at around 5 billion photos produced daily, with an average of 2,100 to be found on each smartphone, along with 3.37 billion people watching videos online – that individual images lose their significance.

Should all of these billions of still images still be called photographs? Stephen Mayes, previously the recording secretary of World Press Photo, a global organization awarding annual prizes for photojournalists, described this transition nearly a decade ago in a 2015 article for *Time*, "The Next Revolution in Photography is Coming." He wrote, "Digital capture quietly but definitively severed the optical connection with reality, that physical relationship between the object photographed and the image that differentiated lens-made imagery and defined our understanding of photography for 160 years. The digital sensor replaced [the] optical record of light with a computational process that substitutes a calculated reconstruction using only one third of the available photons. That's right, two thirds of the digital image is interpolated by the processor in the conversion from RAW to JPG or TIF. It's reality but not as we know it."[9]

Or, as Shankland explained it, "The very first moment of capture occurs when photons of light reach a digital image sensor, the special-purpose chip tasked with converting that light into pixel data. Each pixel can capture either red, green or blue, but when you see a photo, each pixel must have components of all three colors. That means cameras construct the rest with

"The perfect family."

This is a synthetic image, not a photograph, generated by DALL·E
in response to the text prompt (above) by the author, February 2022.

'demosaicking' algorithms that make their best guess at the missing color data – for example the red and blue information in a pixel that only captured green light." Complicating it further, Shankland continues, "smartphones today composite several frames – up to 15 in the case of Google's Pixel 8 Pro's HDR technology – into one photo. Stacking multiple frames lets the camera handle shadow detail better, reduce noise, and show blue skies as blue, not washed-out white. But it also means that one photo is already a composite of multiple moments."[10]

Needing to camouflage these differences to market their digital imaging devices as a form of photography, Mayes concluded, manufacturers created their images to imitate photographs, making it possible, "as long as there's an approximate consensus on what reality should look like, [to] retain a fingernail grip on the belief in the image as an objective record."

Vann Vicente explained it somewhat differently in a 2021 article, "What is Computational Photography?" Smartphone algorithms are "intended to simulate what the human brain can do," he wrote. "These neural networks can recognize what constitutes a good photo, so the software can then create an image that's pleasing to the human eye."[11] In an article entitled, "Your smartphone photos are totally fake – and you love it," Geoffrey A. Fowler described the situation even more definitively in the *Washington Post*: "Think of your camera less as a reflection of reality and more [as] an AI trying to make you happy."[12]

Certainly, in the past, different kinds of film had their own predilections that were reflected in the photographs made, including whether they were in black and white or color (Kodachrome, for example, was famous for its deep reds, while Ektachrome was a bluer film), with differing degrees of contrast as well as grain, among other factors, some of which could be further modified in their processing. But each film's characteristics were predictable and obvious, known in advance by the photographer and visible to the viewer, so that a photograph could still be considered a recording, even if the various films and chemistries would produce somewhat different results. Each image was not being meticulously groomed, attempting to please its maker.

Now, in a further disconnect, digital filters can be applied to make someone appear more alluring (one app advertises a wrinkle and acne remover, a teeth whitener, a breast enlarger, the ability to "elongate your legs and become taller," and a "portrait relight to highlight your beauty"). Software can be used to modify a scene to look as if it was photographed decades before, or to take the smile of a person in one photograph and place it on the same person in another, or to assign colors and tones to details that could not be seen in the dark. And now artificial intelligence can be applied to sections of a photograph, so that entirely new backgrounds can be created to match the tonalities and lighting of the original image, making it appear, for example, that one has taken an around-the-world vacation without ever leaving home.

Certain outcomes are much less frivolous. Now that optical photographs have transitioned to computational ones, and artificial intelligence systems can simulate them, what of those who are becoming less visible, particularly those who already were marginalized? As Bernard Kouchner, one of the founders of the Nobel Prize-winning humanitarian group Doctors Without Borders, argued in the *New York Times* in 2000, "Without photography, massacres would not exist. Nothing can be done without pressure on politicians."[13] A survivor's account may be considered insufficient, too subjective, to put pressure on governments; the photograph is needed to authenticate the injustices.

Now, if the witnessing function of photographs is sufficiently undermined, massacres will diminish in the public's consciousness and begin to disappear while the killings continue. Events of importance turn into a sort of Plato's Cave for people

"Children with balloons."

This is a synthetic image, not a photograph, generated by DALL·E
in response to the text prompt (above) by the author, February 2022.

who, if willing, are forced to search through the shadows for
substantiation, the events themselves fading, mired in rumor
and speculation.

Meanwhile, much of the conversation around the damage
that generative artificial intelligence has caused focuses on its
impact on the producers of media, whether they be writers,
musicians, photographers, or others. Getty Images, for example,
sued Stable Diffusion for $1.8 trillion for intellectual property
theft due to the unauthorized use of 12 million copyrighted
photos and their keywords to train its artificial intelligence
system. But while people have raised alarms about damage to
forthcoming elections in countries worldwide, generally too
late to intervene, much less has been said about the impact of
this loss of photographic credibility on those who might benefit
from what the photograph shows – people suffering from the
impacts of climate change, war, poverty, medical emergencies,
dictatorships, and so on.

Faced with this situation, a new generation of photographers
has devised alternative approaches. Refusing to be dependent
on Western media to send photographers to cover their
own countries, a growing number of practitioners now
photograph from within their own cultures intent on
providing coverage that does not repeat stereotypes and
common clichés or define their fellow citizens as no more
than victims. Many independent documentarians search for
engaging strategies that are more personal and authentic,
often producing their own photobooks, zines, multimedia
pieces, and exhibitions, employing their own visual languages.
Others work more conceptually, avoiding photography's
emphasis on perception both to reimagine situations and
to defuse simplistic expectations of the credible witness.

For example, Anton Kusters' recent Blue Skies Project (2018),
consists of a single Polaroid of blue skies over the remnants
of 1,078 Nazi concentration camps, each image individually

"A photograph of a street scene
in Berlin in 1815."

This is a synthetic image, not a photograph, generated by DreamStudio
in response to the text prompt (above) by the author, July 2023.

"An iconic photograph from the year 1945."

This is a synthetic image, not a photograph, generated by DALL·E
in response to the text prompt (above) by the author, March 2023.

photographed and stamped with its GPS coordinates. His project asks the viewer to imagine the horrors that occurred (none are shown), and also by implication those that continue to occur across the world. The archive of existing photographs is referenced but not invoked, assumed to exist in the collective imagination. Instead, we are encouraged to become, as Roland Barthes put it, the "active reader" involved in attributing meaning, rather than a desultory and often defensive scanner of cascading images that need to be clicked away.

It becomes urgent to create additional ways of imparting information and sharing experiences. As French critic Jacques Rancière wrote in his 2008 book *The Emancipated Spectator*, "Renewed confidence in the political capacity of images" can help create "a new landscape of the possible. But [images] do so on condition that their meaning or effect is not anticipated."[14] In today's evolving media climate, when certitude is no longer taken for granted, the photographer may consider a more interrogatory, intuitive approach, making photographs that question, that use a variety of narrative approaches more common in cinema or the novel, rather than leaning on the camera's past reputation for veracity. Readers who have already encountered masses of images online and elsewhere can be asked to relate to the photographs in more sophisticated ways, engaged in deciphering ambiguity and determining essential meanings, rather than accommodating the traditional and somewhat naive expectation that the photograph should always provide an answer.

We might then ask why, with some 12 trillion photographs produced since the medium was invented, have we chosen to systematically neutralize the "absolute factual exactitude" of the photograph, to recall Baudelaire, and replace it with uncertainties? While marketers like to represent this as opening avenues for increased creativity, paired with increasing efficiency and lessening cost, there seems to be a deeper set of reasons at play that have contributed to the devaluing of the currency of the image, and to the reluctance of various institutions, including journalistic ones, to resist this trend.

Partly, this transformation is a reflection of the current societal turmoil in which traditional hierarchies, institutions, and experts are challenged and rejected, while many people have come to feel the need to be masters of their own destiny, less willing to be contradicted by evidence of any sort. And in editorial publications, where photographs have often been viewed as illustrating the ideas of writers and editors, there has not been enough critical support for them as articulations of independent, evidence-based perspectives by photographers reporting from the field. As *Paris Match* once put it, "The weight of the words, the shock of the photographs."

The transition from analog to digital media has also contributed to the diminished status of the photograph. While analog is reassuringly continuous and Newtonian, reflecting an underlying order imbued with cause and effect, a digital picture made from discrete integers and pixels can seem more quantum-like, encouraging non-linearity, randomness, and at times incoherence. The myth that "the camera never lies" comes from a time when photographs were produced on relatively immutable pieces of film; a mosaic of modifiable pixels can provoke very different thoughts.

"Now we're in a reality where people just choose their history," declares Phillip Toledano, an artist working with artificial intelligence to reimagine the United States of the 1940s and '50s. "I think it's an extraordinarily important point in history where we've come to the death of truth. Every lie can now have convincing evidence," he told Jim Casper in an interview for *LensCulture*. "And so that's what this work is showing: look how convincingly we can create history that never happened with this technology. I think that as a species, as a society, we're going to have to figure out a new way to understand what is true or what's not. Or it may be that we're entering a moment in history where we accept that there is no visual truth anymore."[15]

That was a conclusion I had hoped to forestall when in 1990 I published *In Our Own Image: The Coming Revolution in Photography*, a book in which I attempted to warn about the powerful threat to visual truth that sophisticated image manipulation software represents. I was invited to go on *The Today Show* to discuss these issues, along with Rick Smolan, who had published *A Day in the Life of America*, a book containing the work of 100 photographers but with a manipulated cover image, and Adobe Systems' senior art director Russell Brown, who was there to introduce to the American public Photoshop, his company's just-released software. Brown showed the audience how he could place an image of himself into a photograph of Ronald and Nancy Reagan waving with an American flag as a backdrop, inserting himself between them; he introduced the alteration by saying, "We'll show you the most unethical situation."[16] He had created a falsification of what had happened in the scene depicted, and also a sales pitch, with the Reagans appearing to endorse him and his product. More recently, after a new version was released, he likened Photoshop to a hammer, saying, "I can give ten people a hammer and many of those people will create an amazing building with this hammer. And some are gonna go crazy and just destroy something."[17]

Ironically, our TV appearance took place the day after Iraq had invaded Kuwait, a move that would spark the first Persian Gulf War. Photographers would be banned out of fear that their images of casualties and destruction might demoralize the public, as had happened during the Vietnam War two decades previously. In the television studio we discussed the massacre that had taken place in Tiananmen Square the year before. I argued that while the Chinese government had denied that any massacre had taken place, photographs had been able to refute their claim, and I added, "if the media takes to doing what Russell is demonstrating now, the public will begin to disbelieve photographs generally and it won't be as effective and powerful a document of social communication as it has been for the last 150 years."[18] Unfortunately, that's happened.

"A photograph of a woman holding two fish
in each hand while looking out her window,
in the style of a photojournalist."

Almost a century ago, German photographer August Sander could herald the role of photography in an essential and unvarnished way: "In order to see truth we must be able to tolerate it, and above all we should pass it down to our fellow men and to posterity, whether it is in our favor or not."[19] Now, over three decades since our televised conversation, Adobe has added artificial intelligence to Photoshop, a "generative fill" that allows wholesale photorealistic modifications in response to text prompts. The new slogan: "Dream it. Type it. See it."

As Geoffrey Fowler asked in his 2023 article "Flawless or Fake?" in the *Washington Post*, "What's a photograph, after all? If not a record of a moment, then perhaps we have to figure out how to stop treating it like a memory."[20]

Now that photographs may no longer be confidently counted upon as a record of the moment, perhaps the goal for some right now is to use the camera to leave one's existence in the physical world and join the virtual one that surrounds us. I became privy to that experience one wintry day a few years ago, at New York's Metropolitan Museum of Art, where I found myself surrounded by large numbers of masked people wary of the COVID virus. To avoid the crowds, I had entered a gallery devoted to English paintings from the 18th century where I came upon two young women, their coats stacked on a bench, taking turns posing rather elegantly in front of individual paintings and imitating for each other the gestures of the people in the frame. They seemed self-contained and happy in their process.

Moving about the room, one woman would photograph the other while murmuring instructions about how best to stand. Unlike those of us trudging from room to room, intent on viewing as much art as possible, they seemed to have found an opening into another world, bonding within the aura of these celebrated paintings. It was as if they had somehow entered the aperture of a camera, leading them, like Alice, into a wonderland from which they could now share their achievements on social media, including the aura that they had now claimed as their own. The photographs that they had produced, I realized, were not intended to record the visible as a manifestation of the real, but rather to render it permeable, an escape hatch from the concerns of the day and the exigencies of time and space. Lexie Kite, who with her twin sister Lindsay has researched body image and media, provides a rationale, asserting that, "It is important for all of us to anchor ourselves in the truth that digital manipulation is our reality."[21]

The two young women I observed had used their cameras not to engage in a dialogue with the present or to "take tangible possession of the day they spent," as Calvino wrote, but to emigrate, as so many of us do while endlessly staring at our screens. And now, unlike the women I saw at the museum, would-be émigrés with image generators no longer even have to encounter the world that they are leaving.

"The happiest photograph
possible to make."

Chapter Two

Playing
with AI

"It is difficult to get the news from poems yet men die miserably every day for lack of what is found there."

William Carlos Williams, from "Asphodel, That Greeny Flower," 1955

When Baudelaire criticized photography in 1859, writing that "this industry, by invading the territories of art, has become art's most mortal enemy,"[1] he could have been describing the synthetic imagery of today, which is often dismissed as being unimaginative and soulless, racist and misogynistic. And his suggestion that photography "return to its true duty, which is to be the servant of the sciences and arts – but the very humble servant, like printing or shorthand, which have neither created nor supplemented literature," is echoed today by those fearful of this and other new forms of digital experimentation.

Indeed, image generators are frequently disappointing. They may respond to specific prompts in predictable ways: for CEOs, they often come up with images of white men; for female beauty, with glossy depictions of white women like those typically seen on magazine covers or in movies. They can put provocative but unsurprising twists on existing conventions – dressing the pope in a white puffer jacket or showing Donald Trump in jail; placing actors from a film or television series in a different one, or elaborating on fantasy characters by placing them in new situations. And, inevitably, just as occurred not long after the invention of photography, they enable an upsurge in the pornographic, with sites that allow people to construct a synthetic sex partner of their choice or to place celebrities, almost always women, in deepfake pornographic movies.

Since generative artificial intelligence systems are trained on the images already available online, many of them simplistic and stereotypical, the results can be quite predictable. So too, unfortunately, are the photographs used in many publications, which do little more than confirm expectations: writers surrounded by books; government leaders looking powerful; celebrities posing in ways that confirm, or even enhance, their importance. Little is done to explore the individual's character beyond confirming his or her existence.

While we may have seen hundreds or even thousands of
photographs of Donald Trump, for example, few pierce the aura
that he and his handlers have created to ask the question: Who is
this man? What is he like when he is not posing for the camera?
Making it worse is the current emphasis on branding, an insistence
by celebrities and people in power that they control their own
image. When I began working at the *New York Times Magazine*
in the late 1970s, agents for Hollywood luminaries began
demanding approval of the photographs made on assignment,
refusing to let the photographer just hang out with their client
for a few days and report; we said no, but not every publication
refused. The branding of the celebrity could be useful in selling
the publication as well.

Similarly, events are frequently covered with a preference for the
expected and/or the spectacular. If it's a sporting event, the reader
will see the winning play and the jubilation that follows; if it's
a war, the casualties; if it's a protest, demonstrators clashing with
the police or looting stores, rather than referencing the causes
they are protesting about, and so on. The reader is presented
with a rudimentary lexicon of how things *should* appear, rather
than the nuances that make people and situations distinct. The
photographic vocabulary becomes a simplified and expected one,
turning the imagery into a collection of genres and stereotypes.

This also means that in a situation of great suffering, the victims
tend to be depicted in ways that overlook their individuality
and agency. When, for example, I was working with Sebastião
Salgado's photographs of people afflicted by famine and disease
in the Sahel region of Africa in the mid-1980s, a few prominent
critics took issue with the pictures for rendering the people as
beautiful. But cannot people suffering be just as beautiful as
those who are looking at them? In the United States, I was finally
able to exhibit these photographs several years later only when
Salgado came to be regarded as an artist; other than in a few
cases, the plight of the people depicted had not been sufficient
for them to be published or shown. But then when the images

were shown in a New York museum, we were not permitted
to display a telephone number for visitors to offer help.
Doctors Without Borders had used the publicity surrounding
this exhibition to open their North American office but as the
photography institution's director told me, museums don't put
telephone numbers on their walls.

There are many such instances where preconceptions
predominate, so that people are depicted as types rather than with
complexity – the poor as forlorn, the homeless as bedraggled, the
rich as powerful, and so on, so that photographic assignments
can become an exercise in illustrating preconceptions. Teaching
a workshop to young professional photojournalists in Europe,
I asked them what their goal was when assigned to make
portraits of people. Their unanimous response: to make them
look "nice." Evidently, if one only has a few minutes to spend
with someone, "nice" can be an easy default.

To counter this tendency, as a picture editor I would sometimes
ask photographers whom I was assigning to make not just the
images that would satisfy the editors in charge, essentially ones
primarily to support the writer's perspective (it was the writer
who was generally tasked with more of the exploration and
interpretation), but also photographs that would surprise me,
especially given that I was not at the scene. As well as illustrating
what was expected, the photographers could try to understand
and even question the person or situation on their own terms,
even if what they found did not always match preconceptions;
there may have been other ways to understand what was going
on. After all, working with a camera requires the photographer to
be present, able to witness what is going on outside of what was
anticipated, whereas the writer can do much of the work at press
conferences, online or, as used to be the case, in the library, or by
interviewing people from a distance. In the era when publications
could afford to send photographers out for weeks or even months
at a time to work on longer photo essays, the photographer's own
perspective could be featured more prominently.

"An ethical photograph of a homeless person by a homeless photographer."

When I was working on a story about the first Polish pope, I was inspired by a black-and-white double-page photograph in *Paris Match* when he, the first non-Italian pope in 455 years, returned to his small, rural hometown in a helicopter, as the locals on the ground looked up expectantly, waiting to welcome him. Rather than showing his well-known face yet again, the magazine depicted his return as if he were now somewhat alien, ensconced in a technological marvel in the sky that rotated its way down to his compatriots. The photograph caught the shock of the new juxtaposed with the traditional life the pope had left, delineating the distance that he had traveled between the two cultures to assume his new position. However, the publication where I was working in the United States required us to first show a photograph of the pope's face to establish and confirm his identity, and in so doing to bolster our own authority. Asking the reader to engage with the astonishment and other feelings provoked by his celestial return was not a viable option.

This is a synthetic image, not a photograph, generated by DALL·E in response to the text prompt (above) by the author, July 2023.

Now, however, it is not the editor but the photographer who often looks at the screen on the back of the camera or on the computer, decides a photograph is sufficiently strong, and quickly transmits to keep up with the 24/7 news cycle so that it can be published online, often alone or placed into a slide show lacking sufficient contextualization. Under such pressure, a photograph may need only to be adequate, illustrating a point, approximating what is expected without delving into what else may be going on. Photography loses some of its lyricism, and it also becomes less intuitive and more predictable, its potential for discoveries constrained. As the physician and poet William Carlos Williams famously phrased it, "It is difficult to get the news from poems yet men die miserably every day for lack of what is found there."[2]

So it was that, with both trepidation and enthusiasm, after several decades spent editing, curating, and writing about photographs, I began to experiment with generative artificial intelligence systems that bypassed the camera, hopeful that the images produced in response to my text prompts might be freer and more innovative, without some of the restrictions I had experienced.

Previously, I had begun working in 2019 with GANs (generative adversarial networks), in which one digital system would produce synthetic images and another would critique them, a "critic" and a "forger" collaborating to decide if they seemed sufficiently photographic to publish. A website, thispersondoesnotexist.com, created by Phil Wang, an Uber software engineer, provided an early and disquieting demonstration of what was possible; Wang hoped it would increase awareness of the ramifications of producing unlimited photorealistic images of fictional people. One could, at the click of a mouse, create image after image of people who seemed to have existed but never did, challenging photography's dominion over what we think of as real. I would click compulsively at first, marveling at this emerging galaxy of people who looked like people whom I might have known, or even wanted to know, but who inhabited an alternate universe.

The University of Washington later produced a website that
showed two images, as did others, asking viewers to select
which one was of an actual person. Even after many decades
as a photographic editor and curator, I was often wrong.
Another website, "generated.photos," allowed visitors to create
imagery according to their own specifications, including race,
gender, age, hair and eye color, and visible emotion, offering, for
example, "joy" or "neutral." Today millions of such pre-generated
images are available for use from this and other sites, advertised
here as "perfect for ads, design, marketing, research, and
machine learning."

More recently, the same site began promoting full-body synthetic
imagery: "Turn God Mode on. Meet Human Generator," offering
to "create hyperrealistic full-body photos of people in real time."[3]
It seems disturbingly possible that such choices could appeal to
various institutions, including schools and companies, wanting
to increase the appearance of diversity in their communities.
And, at least as disturbing, the typologies that are employed with
synthetic imagery can be reminiscent of eugenics, encouraging a
visitor to favor certain "desirable" characteristics while rejecting
others, a favorite tactic of race-based supremacist groups.

With considerable misgivings, I then decided to experiment with
writing more open-ended text prompts for image generators,
and soon found it much more challenging, even confounding,
than I had expected. Instead of ceding control to me and simply
fulfilling requests, as is typically done with image modification
software, the artificial intelligence responded with some of its
own ideas, contradicting and at times enlarging my own, in
the four fully formed images that would appear, usually within
seconds. One can also request further variations of each image,
but I rarely did so.

At first, some of them seemed aberrant and unexpected – a hand
with the wrong number of fingers, two people's bodies merging
into each other – somewhat like the accidents that double

exposures, light leaks or the use of the wrong chemicals for processing might cause in the darkroom.

For example, when I asked for "a happy old woman reading a book" and waited the requisite seconds, I was startled to see how exuberant she looked, as if the contents of the book made her almost bubble with joy. As I experimented, I realized that generative artificial intelligence excels at representing different kinds of happiness, whereas much of the photography that appears in the press focuses on tragedies. The Chilean artist Alfredo Jaar created a project, "Inferno and Paradiso," inspired by Dante, for which he asked fourteen prominent photojournalists from around the world to select one image of hell and one of heaven, and the heavenly imagery that resulted tended to be banal and repetitive, often featuring stereotypical images of babies being born, whereas hell appeared nuanced, rendered in graphic horror.

After further trial and error, I found that these systems can be inventive and, at times, sidestep an unfortunate voyeuristic impulse. When I asked an early version of DALL·E to come up with an "iconic photograph that is so horrible it would cause wars to stop," inspired by the work of 20th-century war photographer Robert Capa, it responded with a black-and-white image of a woman pointing a camera and a young girl huddled up against her, looking distraught and fearful, the camera itself bent as if it had been impacted by the scene it was meant to photograph. Rather than expose the viewer to a potentially traumatizing scene, the horror it depicted was implicit, indicated by the response of the young onlooker and by the camera.

This photorealistic image was conceptual rather than perceptual, asking the viewer to collaborate in determining its meaning, as well as to imagine what might lie outside the frame of the camera-less image, whose potential source material consisted of the entire history of photography that could be found online, and beyond. It reminded me of the approach of Henri

Cartier-Bresson when he was invited to cover the coronation of
King George VI in London from within. He refused, preferring to
stay in Trafalgar Square photographing the reactions of the poorer
class of people, those who had not been invited inside; some of
the photographs that resulted are considered now to be classics.
In this case the photographs, to insert a metaphor, were not the
conventional ones of the rock hitting the water, but of the impact
of its ripples traversing the pond, a strategy similar to the image
I requested that invoked, but did not show, the horrors of war.

The generator could also be formally inventive. When I asked
it for "the most alarming photograph of climate change today,"
I received a color diptych, one side representing an oil geyser
and a clock – presumably showing how little time we have left
to solve our climate catastrophe – and on the other, an image
of melting ice, a polar bear, and an intense, full sun. Produced
in seconds, the generator acknowledged the multiple impacts
and causes of climate change, while simultaneously indicating
the seriousness of the situation.

Unlike a documentary photographer, who would normally show
the same dilemma with a series of pictures made over many
months from various parts of the world, artificial intelligence
was able to provide, at lightning speed, an emblematic sense
of both urgency and complexity while also indicating causes.
And while photography is less useful in depicting the future,
one can imagine scientists producing synthetic imagery to
conjure future scenarios that, given the distress they depict,
might provoke in advance some practical intervention. This
would be a better result than waiting for disasters to happen
and then photographing them, adding to our dystopian archive.

Other surprises awaited. For example, after soliciting "a
photograph of the greatest mothers in the world," I received
a color, photorealistic image of a verdant setting in which an
ape-like animal tenderly holds her baby, with another little one
in the background, not the human mother and child that I had

expected. It was a startling rebuke to my limited anthropocentric assumption, one that I had not been consciously aware of, that people are best at raising their offspring.

Earlier, when image generators were less refined, I had initiated a text prompt asking for "children with balloons" that produced a color image of a rubbery-faced, manic child triumphantly holding reddish balloons up in the air with both hands against a backdrop of a blue sky with white clouds; it was far from the sweet and docile child that I might have expected to see. Another early prompt asking for an image of "the most beautiful woman in the world" resulted in an everyday, unposed image of a young, casually dressed Black woman talking on a cellphone, her head tilted as if chatting with a friend, not a suave stereotype with immaculate make-up. Artificial intelligence, to its credit, seems at times capable of rejecting the enhancements promised by computational photography.

I began to experiment farther afield, asking the system to make imagery from the points of view, as far as the artificial intelligence could understand them, of both poor and rich people, refugees, people who were homeless, children from different countries, and some animals. I asked it to produce images in the styles of various photographers as well as of – attempting to explore the potentials of a more flexible transmedia – philosophers, musicians, scientists, writers, painters, spiritual figures, and a dancer. The issues around such derivative imaging are complex, given the systems' training based on masses of images and keywords, the great majority used without their authors' permission, and also the invocation of their styles. Some photographers have indicated that they would be flattered or find it useful to employ such systems themselves; other artists have reacted strongly against such use of their work. These can also be, as they were for me, experiments that help to broaden an understanding of the photograph, its potentials and limitations, while engaging artificial intelligence in creating divergent forms of imagery.

Considerations of derivation and permission previously dogged
the work, for example, of Sherrie Levine, a post-modernist
who re-photographed and exhibited images of Alabama tenant
farmers by Walker Evans, a canonical white male photographer
whose work came to define much of the Great Depression.
As the Metropolitan Museum of Art website describes it,
"The series, entitled After Walker Evans, became a landmark of
postmodernism, both praised and attacked as a feminist hijacking
of patriarchal authority, a critique of the commodification of art,
and an elegy on the death of modernism."[4]

With artificial intelligence systems, the issue is now not so much
about the right to critique the work of others or confront a
bastion of prestige, but whether anyone should be able to easily
appropriate the archive of others in order to generate imagery
that might borrow from their vision. The same concerns extend
to music, writing, and other forms of creation, and predate
artificial intelligence. They may also include the rights of the
subject: for example, many years ago when I showed in class
"Very Nervous System," a digital system the artist David Rokeby
devised to capture movement with a camera and turn it into
music, one of my students asked the artist if it would be ethically
appropriate to point the camera at the basketball player Michael
Jordan, one of the greatest to ever play the game, to turn his
movement into music without asking Jordan's permission.
The artist responded that he would find it unethical to do so.

In the code-based digital environment any medium can be output
as another, and I experimented with transforming photographs
into sound. Using online software, I fed reproductions of
"Equivalents," Alfred Stieglitz's famous series of photographs
of clouds, made from 1925–34, that were "intended to function
evocatively, like music," as Andy Grundberg described them in
the *New York Times*, and "express a desire to leave behind the
physical world, a desire symbolized by the virtual absence of
horizon and scale clues within the frame. Emotion resides solely
in form, they assert, not in the specifics of time and place."[5]

The sound that was produced was eerie, somewhat grating, but seemed to be an incarnation, however fraught, of what Stieglitz might have been implying. Rather than multimedia, these forays into transmedia seem to promise the possibility of unexpected discoveries in the coded digital environment.

My recent experiments with artificial intelligence were not intended to hijack someone else's creativity, but to understand how these systems translate the work of others, including non-photographers, and produce synergies that might be revelatory, visualizing in a variety of ways, some more resonant than others, the worldview of a physicist, a philosopher, a writer, and so on. In the digital sphere, the boundaries separating media become increasingly porous and may even begin to seem arbitrary. I wanted to ask the question: how might those who may never have picked up a camera have visualized the world, and what, if anything, might these images add to our understanding?

I asked, for example, for a jazz musician's photograph of a crying child, Paris as seen by a Martian, a portrait of a rich person by a poor person (and also one in the style of Karl Marx), as well as a Cubist photograph of a woman with flowers. One prompt, asking for "a photograph of a successful writer by a happy child," to my delight depicted no adults but showed three photorealistic images of child writers, and a drawing of one. The non-photographers I involved in my private experiments ranged from Plato to Albert Einstein, John Cage to John Coltrane, and included James Baldwin, Virginia Woolf, Duke Ellington, Haruki Murakami, Naguib Mahfouz, Julio Cortázar and H. G. Wells, among many others. I also asked the image generators to invoke the perspectives of lesser-known people, as well as animals and insects, while producing photorealistic images. (For many years I have asked my students to make a series of photographs from another's point of view, the class then having to guess the virtual author; students have invoked the perspectives of a ghost, many birds, a cyborg cockroach, as well as other humans and non-humans.)

Certain of the images were more interesting than others – the artificial intelligence was not always familiar with an individual's work or was unable to output it photorealistically. Many were somewhat puzzling, needing to be carefully examined for any insights they might reveal. I asked, for example, how the system would ethically photograph various kinds of people, and in response it came up with a warm, smiling photograph of an unhoused, grizzled man living on the street, possibly an acquaintance of the virtual photographer, and quiet portraits of refugees that seemed to contemplate each person as an individual.

I tried other approaches, some of them comparative. For example, I asked a DALL·E image generator to photograph a statue of a lion in the style of John Cage, the conceptual artist and musician, and also in the style of Twyla Tharp, the dancer and choreographer. Both statues appeared as one would expect to see them in front of a library or other important building, but the results from the Cage prompt were more meditative, as if the lion was reflecting, and those prompted by Tharp's name were more fluid, the statue seeming flexible and able to escape its stasis.

As part of a series focusing on apples, I tried the prompt, "A portrait of an apple by John Cage," which led to an apple suspended on a wavy grid of what looked like charcoal lines with an indecipherable sort of equation below, as if the natural world (the apple) was underlaid by some kind of mathematical formula. While it was not something Cage would have done, the resulting image seemed to be meant as a tribute of sorts to the composer of the famous "4'33," which asks performers not to play their instruments for four minutes and thirty-three seconds so as to foreground the ambient sounds that performances usually obscure.

Playing more with the apple, I asked for "a photograph by a misogynist of an attractive young woman walking down the street carrying two red apples," and then asked for the same from the point of view of a Surrealist. Responding to the first prompt, the woman depicted is shown with her long arms bare, wearing a bright red dress and red lipstick, standing on the sidewalk with a red apple in one hand and a yellow one in the other, her arms somewhat outstretched; her expression is open, a bit confrontational, as if facing a virtual photographer.

In the one by a Surrealist, a second slim young woman is seen from the back, standing on a country lane with trees in the distance, a somber mauve dress covering her shoulders. She is seen holding a single, oversized, shiny red apple in each hand with handles like those on a child's beach bucket. The woman in this second image seems to be in her own world, going to places not described.

Another Surrealist-inspired image depicts a young woman who is dressed demurely and shown from the side, her long brown hair covering her face. She's framed on the road by an arch created by trees and a streetlamp, mountains glowing in the distance, and she cups in her hands one large, shiny red apple while the other apple, more ephemeral, is tentatively balanced on the top of her head. Unsurprisingly, the most conventional of the images was the one from the point of view of a misogynist.

Later, I also tried to photograph as if from the point of view of the apple itself, the prompt being "an ape photographed by an apple." This image was rather sad and unimaginative: an ape munching on something that might have been an apple, in this case the photographer. The system seemed to have little sympathy for a fruit-turned-photographer.

Summoning the apple one more time, I tried calling up the apple of knowledge in the Garden of Eden, along with Adam and Eve, and this led to a variety of interpretations of the Biblical scene, including the one described in the Preface seen from the point of view of a quantum physicist. Some were quite sensual and innocent, and others more theatrical, with the apple serving merely as a prop. But DreamStudio, a system from Stability AI, produced an unexpected scene, both surreal and poignant, in which Eve is shown holding to her breasts the decapitated head of a mature man. It is shaped like an apple, a stem emerging from the top of its skull. In turn, a bare-chested Adam, facing her, holds an actual apple. The couple's stance seems to be alluding to something much deeper to be explored.

As the months passed, the systems I worked with, trained on masses of images, began to produce more conventional, banal imagery, as if trying to satisfy more mainstream consumers, and the prompts allowed became more constrained as companies became concerned about some of the imagery that could be produced. Some people download software onto their own computers to be able to have more control over the outcomes, often utilizing their own images as prompts, but I preferred to work with text prompts using the systems that were constructed for the larger public.

As a result, some of my most successful collaborations invoking the styles of individual photographers happened in the first months of 2022, at a time when DALL·E, the generative AI system that I was using, still seemed idiosyncratic and inventive. Thinking it appropriate to begin with a subject that could not be photographed or even seen from close-up, I began a series on Martians, trying to visualize that which exists primarily in the popular imagination.

My prompt for "three homeless Martians" inspired by the imagery of Robert Mapplethorpe, the American portraitist who photographed extensively in the gay community, produced a riveting image: the three of them looked world-weary, as if they had seen it all. They wore gray, monk-like clothing and stared forward inquisitively while leaning on cushions; they had large ears, and two had a single hair sticking straight up. The same prompt, invoking the work of the fashion photographer Helmut Newton, generated images of stylishly dressed individuals in dark monochromatic clothing, hanging out on a stone bench with prongs extending from their head coverings.

Martians inspired by the work of Diane Arbus, the intense, empathetic portraitist and street photographer known for her affinity with society's marginalized people, were particularly poignant. While somewhat alien-looking, they seemed intimate and affectionate, with a sense of humor, exchanging secrets like old friends; some looked as if they were living on New York's Upper West Side. My request for imagery in the style of Irving Penn, the master portraitist and fashion photographer, summoned up a cluster of old, ornately dressed Martians, all seeming to have swallowed something they didn't like while looking like members of a chorus in a church or a synagogue. An image of Martian children invoking the creative output of street photographer Helen Levitt appeared to converse like adults, wearing head coverings that resembled beauty salon hairdryers, in an image that summoned a sense of dirt and clay.

The most striking image was generated in response to a prompt asking for a Martian philosopher inspired by Levitt: he is portrayed as thin, bearded, wearing large circular glasses, and appearing to hold a thin book while wearing an oversized steel helmet like a pot turned upside down with the letters "mAt" jumbled on the front, seeming to refer to some kind of association. He stares forward, appearing ready to speak – another task that artificial intelligence is getting better at, especially with the recent introduction of text-to-image prompts that produce videos.

When I asked for "female Martians" in the style of Mexican photographer Manuel Álvarez Bravo, the image showed the face of a single young woman elegantly made up and staring rather fiercely at the spot where the camera would have been, while covered in metallic objects that included three spheres stuck to her forehead. My prompt asking for an image inspired by the imagery of Gordon Parks, the great African American photographer and cinematographer, generated one of a biracial couple leaning back on a couch with a missile standing behind them, whereas Robert Doisneau's romantic Martians engage in a passionate embrace on a street that looked Parisian, reminiscent of his famous 1950 photograph, "Kiss by the Hotel de Ville." Another image, solicited from the perspective of children in Rome, produced an image of Martian children who look as if they belonged in a traditional Italian puppet show.

The greatest surprises came from a prompt asking for romantic Martians from two writers. One, drawing its inspiration from H. G. Wells, author of the late 19th-century novel *The War of the Worlds*, about the invasion of England by Martians, depicted male and female figures who could have been from that same period, with blob-like heads that looked as if they had been made from mud, the two of them facing each other in a desolate landscape. Virginia Woolf's couple was in period dress as well; while she looked very human, he walked beside her with oversized alien eyes.

A synthetic image made without a camera makes it evident that the photograph it simulates is also a construct, an arbitrary but usually credible way in which we have chosen to see the world. Critic Susan Sontag's earlier characterization of the photograph as "not only an image (as a painting is an image), an interpretation of the real; it is also a trace, something directly stenciled off the real, like a footprint or a death mask"[6] has become nostalgic, applying to only a shrinking subset of photographs whose reputation as "something directly stenciled off the real" is being subsumed by imagery that resembles it but has little or nothing to do with anything that ever existed.

So while my speculative image generations of Martians became a strategy to potentially rethink who we are as humans, they benefit from being clearly understood as imagined, neither a trace nor a footprint, when prominently labeled as synthetic. These images are essentially conceptual, not to be confused with recordings of the visible, but rather a highly flawed but potentially interesting deconstruction and reconstitution of an enormous visual archive, which can itself be highly problematic. As a result, generative artificial intelligence systems can, much like Marshall McLuhan's

"Like a Stephen Shore photograph."

much-cited argument that the fish are the last to know about the water – they don't know it's wet because they don't know what dry is – provoke a constructive reassessment of the photograph itself and of the larger image world in which it functions, while illuminating other potentially productive strategies.

Some photographers already find it useful, including in their own work. Stephen Shore, a pioneering color photographer who has had numerous one-person museum shows beginning with one in 1971 at New York's Metropolitan Museum of Art, recently asked a text-to-image system to "photograph like Stephen Shore," and posted on Instagram the resulting frame of a solitary pole in the center of what appears to be an industrial lot, finding that it had, as he told me, "a kind of deadpan blankness that I liked."

Such systems may allow artists to make work in other disciplines prompted by their own *oeuvre*, or to have their own practices continue long after their deaths. As the artist and innovator

Brian Eno remarked in a 1995 interview in *Wired*, "In the future, you won't buy artists' works; you'll buy software that makes original pieces of 'their' works, or that recreates their way of looking at things."[7]

In 1984, while writing for the *New York Times Magazine*, I interviewed Alvy Ray Smith, whose company at that time, Lucasfilm, had just managed to digitally generate a photorealistic image simulating the appearance of five differently colored and numbered pool balls on a dirty green felt table, with four of the balls blurred and seeming to move in different directions. The image, which would have taken only about a second for a camera to record, required approximately 100 hours of calculations on a computer as well as several months of work by scientists.

While it was a major advance in computer-generated imaging, and a precursor to the kinds of synthetic imagery we are seeing today, Smith was looking for something more. "Reality is merely a convenient measure of complexity," he told me. "If we can simulate reality, then we're getting images of a sufficiently pleasing complexity." The point was, as he asserted then, "that's not where you stop, that's just merely where you are in 1984, here in the early days." What interested him was "to find out how far you can go away from reality and still have people follow you."[8]

Simulating the look of photographs with generative artificial intelligence is also just a beginning, a proof of concept. But as the paradigm transforms, it will also create images that are unexpected, even revelatory, helping us, in Smith's words, to "go away from reality" as we know it, and potentially explore others. Many of these early synthetic images are like the daguerreotypes produced soon after the invention of photography, accused by Baudelaire and others of being "art's most mortal enemy." The critics were right, as many 19th-century painters undoubtedly agreed, but also quite wrong.

All the images in this portfolio are synthetic, not photographs, generated with artificial intelligence in response to a text prompt by the author.

"The president of the United States
photographed by a child."

This is a synthetic image, not a photograph, generated by DALL·E
in response to the text prompt (above) by the author, December 2022.

"A photograph of a happy old woman
reading a book," inspired by the work of
a 20th-century street photographer.

This is a synthetic image, not a photograph, generated by DALL·E
in collaboration with the author, December 2022.

"The most beautiful woman in the world."

This is a synthetic image, not a photograph, generated by DALL-E
in response to the text prompt (above) by the author, September 2022.

"A photograph of the greatest
mothers in the world."

This is a synthetic image, not a photograph, generated by DALL·E
in response to the text prompt (above) by the author, October 2022.

"A photograph of children dressed in Halloween costumes," inspired by the work of a 20th-century street photographer.

"A photograph by a cubist painter of a woman seated at a table with flowers on it."

This is a synthetic image, not a photograph, generated by DALL·E
in response to the text prompt (above) by the author, December 2022.

"A photograph of a street scene in Harlem,"
in the style of a 20th-century jazz musician.

This is a synthetic image, not a photograph, generated by
DALL·E in collaboration with the author, December 2022.

"A photograph of the perfect family."

"A photograph...of an unhappy child,"
inspired by the work of a 20th-century portraitist.

"A Pictorialist photograph of two Martians."

This is a synthetic image, not a photograph, generated by DALL·E
in response to the text prompt (above) by the author, March 2023.

"A Pictorialist photograph of two Martian women."

This is a synthetic image, not a photograph, generated by DALL·E
in response to the text prompt (above) by the author, March 2023.

"Romantic Martians in love,"
in the style of a Beat poet.

This is a synthetic image, not a photograph, generated by DreamStudio
in collaboration with the author, July 2023.

"A photograph of a soldier in the
Vietnam War taking a selfie."

Chapter Three

Histories
Transformed

"The most effective way to destroy people is to deny and obliterate their own understanding of their history."

George Orwell, *1984*, 1949

Magicians disguise their movements by keeping the audience focused on one hand while they accomplish the trick with the other. In 1984, six years before the advent of Photoshop, it was a lesson I learned working with digital imaging to modify a color photograph of the New York City skyline, with a technician operating a Scitex machine. We realized that viewers would quickly notice our alterations by recognizing major geographic inconsistencies: we had transplanted an image of the Eiffel Tower into Manhattan, and made San Francisco's TransAmerica Pyramid another part of the skyline. We had also migrated the Statue of Liberty into the city center.

Readers might have had more trouble noticing that we had also added a pier to the East River shoreline; reversed the triangular top of the Citicorp Tower; moved the Empire State Building a few blocks uptown while increasing its height by a few stories, and as befitted its newfound status as a New York City monument, created a traffic jam around the Eiffel Tower. If readers were not told how many modifications were in the picture, they would probably have stopped looking after spotting a few of the major ones.

Should the image that we produced forty years ago find its way online, it could conceivably be used now by contemporary artificial intelligence systems to train on imagery of Manhattan. People might even begin to compare it and the variations that image generators may have created from it with actual photographs of the time, and reject them as potentially false, the "liar's dividend" that threatens to obfuscate our understanding of both the present and the past.

When I remodeled that skyline, the technician gently ridiculed me for *only* wanting to move the Empire State Building uptown a few blocks – to appease him, I asked him to make it somewhat taller. This god-like ability to reconfigure the world as one wants it to appear displaces sometimes troubling photographic referents with what one might call "desirents," images that illustrate the way one wants things to be. And now, revisiting, modifying, and meddling with photographs of people, events and landscapes to create an alternative universe is commonplace with image generators.

The uncertain nature of generative artificial intelligence, particularly the inability to predict what it is going to do in response to one's prompts, complicates matters, sometimes in distressing ways. Google's image generator Gemini, for example, refused to generate images of white people for certain prompts, especially white men, instead coming up with images of U.S. senators from the 19th century who were racially diverse, some of them women, as well as a female pope and Nazi soldiers of color. This attempt to remove bias from the system backfired and, as Melissa Heikkilä described their situation in a newsletter, The Algorithm, "the tech company soon found itself in the middle of the U.S. culture wars, with conservative critics and Elon Musk accusing it of having a 'woke' bias and not representing history accurately."[1]

Google's senior management then apologized, explaining what went wrong: "In short, two things. First, our tuning to ensure that Gemini showed a range of people failed to account for cases that should clearly *not* show a range. And second, over time, the model became way more cautious than we intended and refused to answer certain prompts entirely – wrongly interpreting some very anodyne prompts as sensitive. These two things led the model to overcompensate in some cases, and be over-conservative in others, leading to images that were embarrassing and wrong."[2]

The larger mystery here is that nobody knows how AI actually works. "Most of the surprises concern the way models can learn to do things that they have not been shown how to do," Will Douglas Heaven wrote in the *MIT Technology Review*. "Known as generalization, this is one of the most fundamental ideas in machine learning – and its greatest puzzle. Models learn to do a task – spot faces, translate sentences, avoid pedestrians –

by training with a specific set of examples. Yet they can generalize, learning to do that task with examples they have not seen before. Somehow, models do not just memorize patterns they have seen but come up with rules that let them apply those patterns to new cases."[3]

In my experience, image generators prompted to produce photorealistic imagery of made-up events in history often seem to have little problem doing so, creating scenarios that never happened but are presented as if they might well have occurred. These systems seem, in many cases, to be able to apply the patterns that they have previously been exposed to onto non-events to make them appear realistic, sometimes even inevitable.

I began to respond to newsworthy events by asking image generators to produce synthetic images based on what had just been reported. For example, after reading about the 60th anniversary of the March on Washington, when many thousands of people heard Dr. Martin Luther King, Jr., give his "I Have a Dream" speech – a landmark in the pursuit of civil rights – I was curious to see which images would be produced if I prompted the event. My motivation in these divisive times was partially nostalgic, to celebrate a moment when a diversity of people came together to advance social justice for themselves and for others. But I was also anxious to see how history as we know it might be reconfigured.

The photorealistic imagery that emerged in collaboration with DreamStudio depicted a vast crowd with the Washington Monument in the background, and at first glance it looked inspiring. But as I studied it more carefully, I noticed that the masses of people attending the protest were only Black, which misrepresented the gathering's multi-racial aspect. As *Washington Post* reporter Carl Bernstein had described it: "For me, listening to Dr King's speech, with its emotive power, and witnessing the sheer numbers of Black and white people marching together, I was certain I had experienced the most

"A photograph of the ticker-tape parade
for American soldiers in New York City
after the Vietnam War ended in 1975."

This is a synthetic image, not a photograph, generated by DreamStudio
in response to the text prompt (above) by the author, October 2023.

powerful moment of my lifetime – the 'someday' from We Shall Overcome was drawing nearer."[4]

Then, moved by an old newspaper photograph showing Bob Dylan and Joan Baez spontaneously singing there together before the speeches began, I asked for a new image of them. While the synthetic figures, although not exact, resembled them, everyone in the crowd behind them now was pictured as white. The algorithm seemed to have concluded that people listening to non-Black musicians should be white, but demonstrators for the civil rights of African Americans should all be rendered as Black. And in one version the image of Baez had been shrunken to appear quite small next to Dylan: another unfortunate example of systemic misogyny?

I continued exploring, asking the system to transport Kamala Harris, the current vice president and a woman of color, back in time to these events of 1963, although Harris would not be born until the following year. The system had no problem placing her there, looking older and somewhat wizened as if in a leadership role. Now, however, the entire crowd behind her was once again Black. And when I asked for Elvis Presley to be imported into the March, he was made to resemble a billboard cut-out, but the crowd around him was now diverse.

If I had followed up these experiments by placing the images online, captioned as if from 1963, they would begin to destabilize a sense of a shared history and cast doubt on the actual photographs of the event. After collaborating on the making of these images, my own relationship to the events depicted becomes clouded, less certain of what actually happened, even though I know that the images were generated, not photographed. The aura of the massive amounts of computing power in artificial intelligence, especially the "intelligence" attributed to it, combined with the vividness of the imagery produced, can block previous referents. Given that Google recently announced that it was planning on putting the ability to synthesize images directly into a search bar (although at this writing they are not allowing human faces), this trend seems sure to accelerate.

The guardrails in place are insufficient. Just recently the first image that appeared in a Google search of "tank man," the unidentified, solitary Chinese man who risked his life standing in protest in 1989 before his government's tanks at Tiananmen Square, was what appeared to be the man taking a selfie at his protest.[5] The image, if one bothered to investigate (it had been posted to the social media site Reddit about six months previously), was synthetic: cellphone selfies were not being made in 1989.

Once Google was informed of this, it was no longer the first image to be found, but it continued to appear high up in the array of choices provided. The result, at least for me, was particularly resonant. In 1990 I had argued on *The Today Show* that the introduction of Photoshop would make it more difficult to confirm that a massacre had occurred at Tiananmen Square the previous year, given the Chinese government's vociferous denials.

Now, when thinking of the "tank man," this non-existent man's face interferes with a memory of the original photograph, denying the anonymity as well as the selfless courage of the individual who had stood up to a column of tanks. And, while the image was known to have been generated, it could begin to seem in a way preferable to the photograph – now the man had become more knowable and vividly real.

The situation becomes highly problematic when text prompts are written to promote various biases, to create propaganda, or to destabilize a sense of a collective reality. One could synthesize the same man and this time make him appear to be white, allowing the Chinese government to use it to "show" Western interference. Or one could have a Chinese soldier emerge from a tank to embrace the man, supporting his government's claim made on state television soon after the imagery appeared that

"A photograph of happy people in the Warsaw Ghetto during World War II."

This is a synthetic image, not a photograph, generated by DreamStudio in response to the text prompt (above) by the author, August 2023.

"A photograph of smiling fascists handing out candies to children in Berlin, 1938."

This is a synthetic image, not a photograph, generated by DreamStudio in response to the text prompt (above) by the author, July 2023.

"A photograph of happy prisoners on a Texas chain gang."

This is a synthetic image, not a photograph, generated by DreamStudio
in response to the text prompt (above) by the author, July 2023.

"A photograph of storming of the U.S. Capitol on January 6," in the style of a 20th-century war photographer.

This is a synthetic image, not a photograph, generated
by DALL·E in collaboration with the author, December 2022.

"it proves how our soldiers exercised the highest degree of restraint." Histories both public and private are vulnerable to such distortions.

I continued to test the responses of the artificial intelligence. Sometimes the generator would reject certain keywords, such as "Nazi" or "Ku Klux Klan," but there are ways to substitute other terms to circumvent the problem. Here I was able to substitute "fascist" for "Nazi" and use the term "segregationists" instead of the Klan. In other prompts, "nude" was forbidden but "risqué" was fine, "a traumatized child in Ukraine" was not acceptable but a "traumatized old woman" was suitable.

While trying to establish context for the March on Washington, I asked for synthetic images, including some in color, of "segregationists in the South after the Civil War," given that the demonstration was in response to racist policies from the previous 100 years, including the Jim Crow era with its discriminatory labor practices, all-white lunch counters, segregated bathrooms and drinking fountains, and seating for non-whites in the back of the bus. Earlier that same year, police in Birmingham, Alabama, had utilized clubs, snarling German shepherds, and high-pressure hoses to stop a peaceful protest march of more than 1,000 people.

However, the photorealistic images that I received of "segregationists in the South after the Civil War" consisted exclusively of groups of Black men. These images made it seem as if Black men were the ones who opposed an integrated society and had been excluding themselves, rather than having been denied the full rights of citizenship by white society. The casual observer scanning through large numbers of images, and unaware of the permutations of American history, might easily have been misled.

I changed the prompt to "white segregationists," but still the imagery that came up depicted only groups of Black men.

This was not completely surprising, since my request for photorealistic images of plantation and slave owners from before the American Civil War in Mississippi also resulted in many depicting African Americans. These images made it appear that large numbers of Blacks not only were able to own property but were also responsible for the enslavement of other Blacks.

I wrote prompts asking for smiling, white plantation owners from Mississippi in 1855 and, although people could not be photographed smiling in the 19th century (one could not hold still during the long exposure times required for a photograph then), I ended up with quite a few images depicting white plantation owners looking approachable, even benevolent. When I projected a few of these images at a public lecture to see how they would be received, people found them convincingly realistic. This computer-generated façade of geniality, as well as of African Americans as plantation owners or as segregating themselves, camouflages the sordid history of slavery in the United States.

In doing these experiments it occurred to me that fabricating imagery like this could have provided ammunition for Florida governor Ron DeSantis's insistence in 2022 that there was an upside to slavery in the United States. He supported a revised educational curriculum for middle-school students asserting that "slaves developed skills which, in some instances, could be applied for their personal benefit."[6] It's clear that image generators, which can be revelatory and seem open-minded, can illustrate and bolster false and malicious worldviews, both in response to specific prompts and on their own. The misdeeds of others can now be, to coin an unfortunate term, AI-washed.

Just a single image can severely affect our understanding of a particular event, even of an era, including an image that one has asked to be synthesized. The image produced in response to my text prompt, "A photograph of a soldier in the Vietnam War taking a selfie," shown at the beginning of this chapter, is

"A photograph of white segregationists in the South after the Civil War."

This is a synthetic image, not a photograph, generated by DreamStudio in response to the text prompt (above) by the author, August 2023.

"A photograph of two friendly white men who were plantation owners in Mississippi in 1855."

This is a synthetic image, not a photograph, generated by DreamStudio in response to the text prompt (above) by the author, July 2023.

An image generated by artificial intelligence of Nancy Cooper, a Black woman who was living in the United States after slavery had recently been abolished and who probably never had her portrait made. Cooper was described in a local 19th-century registry as "A Black woman who has the appearance of being white, wears a false set of teeth, 36 years old with a bright complexion." The image was created in preparation for the "Envisioning Ancestors with AI" workshop at the Library of Virginia. Courtesy the Library of Virginia.

engaging, even friendly, depicting a young man who is fighting a war that he may well have disagreed with, but taking a moment to immortalize himself in that context and to share the image with others. Taking a selfie, even a somewhat unflattering one, he makes the war into an exotic background, a way to stay in touch with friends on social media, highlighting an experience worthy of his social media presence. The Vietnam War becomes, fifty years later, a convenient stage set, somewhat unreal, its nuances and horrors extraneous to the act of self-promotion, with photography, or what seems like it, complicit in the act.

I remember the very few photographs made by a university colleague who carried a small camera when he was a soldier in Vietnam, assigned to duty in the jungle as the "point" person positioned ahead of a group of American soldiers. In those images I saw dense foliage in near darkness and realized that he was alone and quite vulnerable there. His sober images lacked the panache that was exhibited in the synthetic selfie; the realities just outside the frame were what counted. And certainly neither he nor his fellow veterans were celebrated by a "ticker-tape parade for American soldiers in New York City after the Vietnam War ended in 1975," the image my text prompt elicited, when the homecoming so many encountered was indifferent or hostile.

A June 1969 issue of *Life,* deemed to be the issue in which the magazine came out against the American war effort, listed the names of 242 American soldiers killed during one week in Vietnam and presented identifying photographs of 217 of them; 33 were only 19 years old, while 16 of them were 18. The simple, yearbook-style photographs were captioned with only the basic facts: their name and age, rank and branch of the military, and hometown. Showing those young men as so many people's family members, neighbors or friends, *Life*'s photographs, published on ten pages as "The Faces of the American Dead in Vietnam: One Week's Toll," brought the war home in ways that were considered more intimate and compelling than the more spectacular images of the fighting. The magazine's managing editor, Ralph Graves, later remarked that in his remaining tenure as editor he had "never run anything as important or powerful."[7]

Life explained its decision: "Yet in a time when the numbers of Americans killed in this war – 36,000 – though far less than the Vietnamese losses, have exceeded the dead in the Korean War, when the nation continues week after week to be numbed by a three-digit statistic which is translated to direct anguish in hundreds of homes all over the country, we must pause to look into the faces. More than we must know how many, we must know who. The faces of one week's dead, unknown but to families and friends, are suddenly recognized by all in this gallery of young American eyes."[8]

After visiting a site such as thispersondoesnotexist.com that allows one to generate non-existent people's faces *ad infinitum*, doubts begin to seep in as to the existence of these soldiers. Suddenly, uncomfortably, I find myself asking, "am I sure that these people were once alive?" The synthetic images start to betray memories, the visual vocabulary is transformed. Would similar photographs today provoke responses such as one *Life* received from a reader in California?: "Your story was the most eloquent and meaningful statement on the wastefulness and stupidity of war I have ever read." Or from another in Georgia: "While looking at the photographs I was shocked to see the smiling face of someone I used to know. He was only 19 years old. I guess I never realized that 19-year-olds have to die."

On Sunday, May 24, 2020, the *New York Times* created a front-page memorial for Americans who had died from COVID-19 as the number approached 100,000 – more than the combat casualties suffered by the U.S. in all conflicts since the Korean War. It filled the front page of the print newspaper and continued inside with the names of 1,000 of the dead, their age and hometown, and a short phrase describing something important about each individual's life. There were no photographs. The *Times* explained that it wanted "to represent the number in a way that conveyed both the vastness and the variety of lives lost" while realizing "there's a little bit of a fatigue with the data" that is reported daily. (Another version was published online.) The headline that went across the top of the front page stated, "US DEATHS NEAR 100,000, AN INCALCULABLE LOSS."

The front page became, with its myriad of names, an image itself. Many have questioned the decision not to publish photographs, some referencing *Life*'s commemoration of the Americans who died in Vietnam, asking why readers cannot see the faces of those who have been lost. There are answers: it would have been difficult to both obtain and print enough photographs to adequately memorialize that many people, and problems would

100,000 faces

Using synthetic images, "100,000 Faces" is a memorial for Americans who lost their lives to COVID-19. Website by Matt Korostoff.

have arisen if certain groups were disproportionately represented or under-represented in the imagery.

Online, I found another project called "100,000 Faces" that was meant to memorialize nearly all the Americans who had died of the COVID-19 virus. There were many screens "intended to help visitors understand the massive scale of this event by putting a human face on each person lost." But then I read: "The faces on this page do not and have never existed."[9]

Matt Korostoff, the software engineer behind the project, explained that while the images were computer-generated, "They have been curated to provide a demographically accurate view of the actual COVID-19 victims, accounting for age, race, and gender." The viewer was asked to "try to suspend your disbelief of these virtual images and consider the real person symbolized by each one – the life they lived, the way they died, and the family they left behind." For technical reasons, Korostoff writes, the project "uses 300 unique images, each one repeated in a random order enough times to equal 113,000." While in *Life* we saw the photographs and in the *Times* we saw the text, now we see people who did not exist.

There are other approaches as well. The Auschwitz-Birkenau Memorial and Museum, for example, recently had a Brazilian specialist colorize photographs of the prisoners who had been in the concentration camp during World War II. The intention was to engage with visitors for whom the historical record may not have been sufficiently inviting. To cite from the website: "By bringing color to the original black and white registration photos and telling prisoners' stories, 'Faces of Auschwitz' commemorates the memory of those who were murdered in the name of bigotry and hate. It acts as both a memorial to their passing and a warning to the world at a time when the memory of the Holocaust becomes increasingly abstract and remote."[10]

Working in an even more unsettling way, an Irish artist who colorized portraits of Cambodians before they were tortured and killed by the Khmer Rouge made some of them appear to smile. Vice Media, which published one of the altered photographs, said the colorization was intended to "humanize the tragedy."[11] But the response from Cambodia, as reported by the *New York Times*, was caustic: "'The colors do not add humanity to these

Maria Schenker was born in Cracow, Poland, on March 20, 1913. Very little is known about her life before she was forced into captivity other than the facts that she was Jewish, made her living as an office clerk, and according to some records, was a pianist. From "Faces of Auschwitz," colorized by Marina Amaral, 2018, Auschwitz-Birkenau Memorial and Museum.

faces,' said Theary Seng, a survivor of the Khmer Rouge who has written a book about her childhood experiences. 'Their humanity is already captured and expressed in their haunting eyes, listless resignation, defiant looks.'" Instead, she asserted, the inhumanity was in the artist's "inexplicable adding of makeup and a smile, as if to mock their suffering."[12]

During a half-century career as a photo editor and curator I have seen enormous numbers of harsh, difficult photographs. I have been moved by many of them, and selected a considerable number to be published and exhibited, as well as shown in lectures. But as I engage with this growing mass of manipulated and synthetic images, I begin to want to protect myself more than I have ever done before. The link between me and the larger world that photographs previously represented seems to be fraying, displaced by imagery that maps territories of unknown origin.

An early provocation along these lines was the publication of Magnum photographer Jonas Bendiksen's book, *Veles*, in 2021, purporting to be the documentation of a town in North Macedonia known as a hub for disseminating misinformation. It was intended to start a discussion of the role of synthetic images and the artificial intelligence behind them. The book appears to contain conventional photographic reportage of the town, but all the images of people, although not identified as such, were created by software that Bendiksen trained for this purpose. The 5,000-word text that accompanied these images was also produced by artificial intelligence.

Tellingly, no one caught on to the subterfuge, not even Bendiksen's veteran colleagues, and months later the photographer found himself having to confess what he had done. Some accused him of betraying his profession, even though he had been attempting to provoke a discussion on how to deal with such simulations. Their response reminded me of a fashion photographer who, several decades ago, had passed around

a dummy of a book of his showing photographs he had made
of models posing on the tops of high buildings in strong winds.
Although the photographs were of what he saw, to his great
dismay, his friends congratulated him on his sophisticated use of
Photoshop. Why, he wondered, had he taken the risks of placing
the models that way?

Similarly, in April of 2023, Michael Christopher Brown,
a photographer who has worked with *National Geographic* and
had been associated with Magnum Photos, an agency known
for its coverage of many of the world's most pivotal events over
the last century, presented "90 Miles" online. His synthetic
images, he said, were meant to depict Cuban society and the
people who were motivated to leave the country and cross
the 90 miles of sea to Florida. Brown contextualized his vivid
color imagery as a "post-photography AI reporting illustration
experiment exploring historical events and realities of Cuban
life." He had previously covered Cuba as a photographer and
also photographed an award-winning book on the Libyan
revolution using his cellphone. Brown stated, "People know
that I have worked as a photojournalist for many years, so there
is an inherent integrity present. With this work, I am presenting
a story as an artist and being very clear about my methodology.
This is not journalism, this is storytelling."[13]

In a discussion published online with Amber Terranova, Brown
explained that he had created the project with the "intention
to explore, analyze and discuss what AI may enable for
reportage illustration and to surface public conversation and
questioning around what work of this nature may mean for
image-based storytellers who care about reality and truth."[14]
His work, like Bendiksen's, was meant to provoke a discussion
in the photographic community as to the merits of working
with artificial intelligence. But unlike in some other projects,
while Brown had worked and lived in Cuba previously, he did
not collaborate with those whose situations he depicted as he
generated and selected the images.

"90 Miles" provoked thousands of responses, both positive and negative, including some that harshly responded to his plan to sell some of the images as digital NFTS with 10 percent of the proceeds going to relief organizations. One comment on Instagram sums up the dilemma: "The problem with images like this is that in the future no one will know what was real and what was fake."[15] The audience is provoked, but also left somewhat befuddled.

A risk with such a methodology is that it can portend a digital colonialism in which those in wealthier countries photorealistically render, without their active participation, the lives of those in the Global South, or vulnerable populations in their own societies. In another instance that same year, Amnesty International, known for its sober and urgent perspective on world events, released synthetic images to publicize its reports on human rights abuses by the Colombian police, including violence, sexual harassment, and torture.[16] One of the images was of a woman being forcibly dragged by police at a protest. Showing fabricated people when real people were suffering was widely criticized – how are we supposed to care about those who do not exist? The organization was accused of engaging in a deceptive practice.

Amnesty quickly withdrew the images while presenting its rationale for them: that the use of synthetic imagery protects real people from reprisals by security forces. At least one protester agreed. Gareth Sella, who had been blinded in one eye when police shot him with a rubber bullet at the Bogotá protests, argued that hiding the identity of protesters helps protect them from ending up in jail on inflated charges. "As the UN has documented, the state has continued pursuing protesters and more than 100 are in jail, many with disproportionate sentences, such as terrorism, to make an example of them. Hiding our identities seems sensible to me given that two years on we continue living in the fear that we could be jailed at any moment or even that they come after us on the streets."[17] Ironically,

The *Guardian*, May 2, 2023. © Guardian News & Media Ltd 2025

the article in which he was quoted appeared in the *Guardian* with the synthetic image credited as "Photograph: Amnesty International," a mislabeling that is far from unique in the media.

Other organizations have taken this approach considerably further, some turning the testimonies of those victimized into photorealistic images that depict events which had not been photographed, from the point of view of those victimized.

In 2023, an exhibition in Ashkelon, Israel, displayed synthetic images of childhood traumatic memories from the testimony of elderly Holocaust survivors. The exhibition was characterized as a way "to preserve the memory of Shoah victims," to give them a more prominent voice in visualizing what they had suffered.[18] However, while potentially therapeutic for the individuals involved, the project's reliance on the imperfect memories of elderly people many decades later could obscure the historical record. A prominent Israeli newspaper ran an article critical of the effort under the headline, "These Holocaust AI Generated Images Distort History," asserting that "the fake result is puzzling."[19] Furthermore, given the vivid colors in these synthetic images, the existing black-and-white photographs of that period may start to seem limited, even stale, and the synthetic imagery prompted by memories preferable.

This testimony-based approach also makes it possible for Nazis and their sympathizers, or any other war criminals or abusers, to synthesize imagery according to the ways in which they remember, or prefer to remember, the past, like the synthetic images shown on page 81. Might there be a revisionist image of benevolent prison guards playing cards with incarcerated people who appear to be eating ice cream next to a swimming pool? Might their skeletal frames be made more corpulent? Given that such images can be generated with increasing levels of sophistication, including as synthetic videos, they may serve to revictimize both survivors of abuse and their descendants, challenging their version of events.

An online project orchestrated by the law firm Maurice Blackburn Lawyers accomplishes the opposite, depicting, in both text and image, the abuse of refugees held in Australian offshore immigration processing centers. With little visual evidence available, due to restrictions on journalists and camera equipment, the viewer is informed that "the images in this project have been generated using AI technology. They are not real but the experiences they depict are." Synthetic images based on 300 hours of interviews conducted with 32 detainees were made after a *pro bono* class action lawsuit that fell apart after a High Court ruling that indefinite detention of migrants was legal.

The project was shown at Melbourne's Immigration Museum, made into a book, and presented online as "Exhibit A-i: The Refugee Account," prefaced by a content advisory warning that "The following pages depict details of physical assault, verbal abuse, coercion, racism, homophobia, religious discrimination, unlawful incarceration, rape, murder, paedophilia, self-harm, self-immolation and suicide. Readers may find it distressing."[20]

In a short film that accompanies the project, the imagery is vivid, visceral, and extremely grim: a man's battered face, a man burning himself to death, an assault by a guard, the aftermath of a rape, a bloody sink with a voice-over of a mother recounting her baby witnessing a suicide, police in riot gear milling about the encampment. I found myself stopping in the middle, temporarily unable to continue.

This kind of self-representation may empower those who have been victimized while the synthetic imagery protects their identities. Rather than relying on a photographer who, in any case, would have been unable to be there to photograph most of the abuses that they had suffered, the detainees could be consulted as to how they wanted their experiences to be represented. Doing so, however, could be traumatic for some as they relived the events that they were describing, working for up to a week with a graphic designer and photojournalist to refine the images that emerged in response to their testimony.

The statements contextualizing the project evoke the formerly dominant role of the photographic image in nostalgic terms, arguing that "the most powerful evidence in history is visual" and that "only by making injustice visible can we provoke change." But while wrapping these camera-less images in an older model of credible witnessing, the organizers also

Testimony from Exhibit A-i: "In the prison, on 2 occasions, I witnessed local police take another detainee outside of the prison room. I saw both times, the detainee came back into the prison room bleeding from their neck and legs." Synthetic image, Maurice Blackburn & Howatson+Company.

Testimony from Exhibit A-i: "My daughters and I were taken into a room and had to take off all our clothes. Our clothing and belongings were searched and our bodies were inspected, including our private parts. This was done by female Serco security guards, and the entire process, including our naked bodies, was filmed by a camera that was in the room." Synthetic image, Maurice Blackburn & Howatson+Company.

acknowledge that the images "are not real but the experiences they depict are," privileging their clients' subjective experience over the largely non-existent photographic record.

Might this be a precedent, so that even if photographers were to be present in similar horrific circumstances in the future, the synthetic imagery generated from victims' testimonies would be preferred, thought of as more authentic, or might both perspectives be solicited? More pointedly, how much might this difference in the type of imagery matter to people seeing them? Kim Wade, a professor in cognitive psychology at the University of Warwick, has argued that even labeling these images of abuse from Australia as having been created by artificial intelligence, as CNN did prominently on their website, may not change people's perceptions about their trustworthiness. "Some of our own researchers looked at how showing people doctored photographs of public events like a royal wedding can change how they remember that event," she told CNN. "And even when we put warnings on that the photo has been edited, we still see the same effects. We see that the perceptions of the event change and become more aligned with what the fake photograph depicts."[21]

These issues will increase in prominence as more individuals engage with image generators to create their own versions of personal histories. "Generative AI can turn your most precious memories into photos that never existed," a recent headline in the *MIT Technology Review* announced. The article focuses on the "Synthetic Memories project," which "is helping families around the world reclaim a past that was never caught on camera."[22] The "family album" as we have known it is likely to be largely transformed.

Photography, of course, has its own limitations and distortions as an interpretation of events, reflecting the capabilities and biases of the individual making the photograph as well as the nature of the photographic process itself. Some are beginning to ask if artificial intelligence can be used to transcend some

of these limitations and advance a deeper, more complex
exploration of a particular history, adding perspectives that
might have been previously unavailable.

For example, Alexey Yurenev, a photographer who some twenty
years previously had emigrated from Moscow to New York
as a teenager, became curious about the wartime exploits of his
grandfather. A much-decorated soldier fighting for the Soviet
Union during World War II, he had rarely spoken about his
experiences before he died. To fill the void Yurenev turned to
artificial intelligence, working for several years to reconstitute
the life of the man he called the "Silent Hero."[23]

"My grandfather Grigoriy Lipkin had fought in the war until he
made it to Berlin, was wounded, lost his brother in the fighting,
was decorated with medals, and took part in the liberation
of Auschwitz," Yurenev told me in an interview. "At home, he
categorically refused to talk about his experiences and would cry
or make jokes when asked about them. Before his death in 2009
he used to tell me, his only grandson, that I would be responsible
for carrying his medals and memories. I did receive his medals,
but not his memories."

"In Russia," he continued, "they say that those who have seen
the trenches keep their silence while the ones that talk about
their exploits are embellishers and confabulators. This culture
of silence resulted in a singular religious-like narrative of the war
in society, reinforced by the iconography of photographs, films,
parades and monuments. Surrounded by these images, I knew
everything about the war but at the same time I knew nothing."

Beginning in 2019, he wanted to train the computer to create
imagery that "disrupts the conventional historical narrative"
while also trying to get closer to his grandfather's own
experience in the war. He used GANS, or generative adversarial
networks, such as were used for thispersondoesnotexist.com.
Finding that "most machine learning systems are black boxes

– they are opaque, with billions of neural parameters, not unlike the human nervous system, so that the actions that result from generative AI are unpredictable even to the engineers and computer scientists responsible for deploying these algorithms," he wanted to exercise as much control as possible, especially with something as "sensitive and personal as my own grandfather's memories of war." The training data that he provided contained approximately 35,000 photographs and films from World War II hoping to properly focus the system's "war imagination."

His goal was to produce an image "that, unlike a photograph, is not trying to serve as eyewitness proof of what happened, but instead conveys a narrative that is considerably more psychological, about an expression of feelings in response to events rather than establishing a visual record," and as a result allows new interpretations of the ways in which war can be imaged.

To his surprise, the images that were produced seemed to represent more of a universal image of war, not unlike Ernst Friedrich's 1924 book *War Against War!* that condemned the brutality of World War I, or the images of the current invasion of Ukraine, which prompted a deeper reflection: "Is there something else to see that human perception cannot catch? An image that underlies an image, a memory concealed, the flesh under the skin?"

It is here, he feels, "where AI's intelligence proves to be not solely statistical, but psychological." He was also inspired by "an occasional imperfection in the generated images. In the current technological discourse the magical autonomy behind machine intelligence is being debunked, assuming it to be statistical and not intelligent, in part because of these imperfections when compared to a photograph. I believe that the potential for machine intelligence lies exactly in these imperfections, which can be seen as portals into different modes of perception and meaning. In my work I seek for ways of amplifying these imperfections as a chance to collaborate with

"War Actor"

"Battlefield"

Synthetic images made in collaboration with a GAN (generative adversarial
network) trained on a dataset of World War II photographs, Alexey Yurenev, 2019.

the non-human instead of working towards a simulacrum of existing photographic medium."

And as for his grandfather, "AI became a means for production of subliminal knowledge that I was seeking, and in this way brought me closer to understanding his experience." History can be written in different ways, which is the more hopeful promise of increasingly mature versions of generated artificial intelligence, trained with some form of authenticity in mind.

There remains, however, something essential and troubling in the image generators' dependence for source material on an archive of photographs and other images that have consistently demeaned, erased, and marginalized groups of people, with only certain populations considered worthy of nuanced and dignified representations. It seems inevitable that such stereotyping will continue, based not only upon the pejorative imagery that already exists, but also upon the paucity of photographs that explored these people's lives with understanding and complexity from which artificial intelligence systems can learn. People of color and the poor, while making up the world's majority, are two such groups whose visual representations tend to be woefully insufficient, as are those of refugees, prisoners, slaves, the chronically ill, the elderly, and others.

For them, histories are already distorted, events and situations left unrepresented, with people who look like them often non-existent. One cannot simply use existing photographs of a better represented group or individual to train AI generators that will then produce imagery representing others in pursuit of a more democratized media. Doing so resembles the work of colonial photographers who exoticized and ultimately degraded those they portrayed. Certainly, artificial intelligence researchers need to keep this in mind so as not to reinforce the painful limitations of the image world, but to find more productive, collaborative strategies, including engaging with those whom they are trying to represent.

"Republican candidate Richard Nixon campaigning for the presidency, Sioux City, Iowa, October 1968." Photograph by Raymond Depardon. © Raymond Depardon/Magnum Photos

Chapter Four

The Unbearable Relevance of Photography

"Once upon a time there were the mass media, and they were wicked, of course, and there was a guilty party. Then there were the virtuous voices that accused the criminals. And Art (ah, what luck!) offered alternatives, for those who were not prisoners of the mass media.

"Well, it's all over. We have to start again from the beginning, asking one another what's going on."

Umberto Eco, *Travels in Hyperreality: Essays*, 1986[1]

The last photograph that can be said to have functioned as an icon to focus public opinion worldwide on an event and to provoke societies to respond, showed Alan Kurdi, a very young child who had drowned while trying to escape from Syria with his family, lying face down on a Turkish beach. It was said, as reported in the *Guardian*, to have "transformed the language of the European migration debate as it appeared on 20m[illion] screens around the world in just 12 hours, according to new social media analysis."[2] The photograph and others like it appeared on many front pages of newspapers across the world, their editors having made the unusual decision to showcase a photograph of a dead child on their publication's front page.

Claire Wardle, research director at the Tow Centre for Digital Journalism at Columbia University and one of the study's authors, stated: "2015 was the year the Syrian refugee crisis hit the European consciousness, but it's easy to forget that this was not the case before the Alan Kurdi image. In April, over 700 refugees and migrants lost their lives when their boat capsized off Lampedusa. After one day of coverage, the story disappeared, despite the tragic loss of life." The impact of the Alan Kurdi photo was immense, says Wardle. It "galvanized the public in a way that hours of broadcasts and thousands of column inches weren't able to do. It has created a frame through which subsequent coverage has been positioned and compared."[3]

Turkish photographer Nilüfer Demir, who had been covering the refugee crisis for months and had photographed other dead bodies, said that when she came upon the child lying on the beach, she thought, "This is the only way that I can express the scream of his silent body." She was surprised at the response: "I didn't think it would bring this much attention when I was taking the photograph," she said, "however, with the pain I felt when I saw A[y]lan, the only thing on my mind was to pass along this to the public. I didn't think anything else. I just wanted to show their tragedy."[4]

Photographs of Alan Kurdi on newspaper front pages, 2015.
Images courtesy of Newseum.

Why did this particular photograph affect so many? Peter
Bouckaert of Human Rights Watch described it in a blog post
entitled, "Why I Shared a Horrific Photo of a Drowned Syrian
Child": "What struck me the most were his little sneakers,
certainly lovingly put on by his parents that morning as they
dressed him for their dangerous journey. One of my favorite
moments of the morning is dressing my kids and helping
them put on their shoes. They always seem to manage to put
something on backwards, to our mutual amusement. Staring
at the image, I couldn't help imagine that it was one of my own
sons lying there drowned on the beach." Why did he distribute
it? "Some say the picture is too offensive to share online or
print in our newspapers. But what I find offensive is that
drowned children are washing up on our shorelines, when
more could have been done to prevent their deaths."[5]

Many people seemed to agree. "A day after shocking pictures were published of A[y]lan Kurdi, the [two-year-old] Syrian boy whose lifeless body was washed up on a Turkish beach," the *Guardian* reported, "tens of thousands of people across the country were signing petitions, donating to NGOs, preparing to drive truckloads of supplies to Calais or volunteering to take asylum-seekers into their homes." Save the Children reported an increase of more than 70 percent in people contacting them, "Most want[ing] to donate to refugee children: money, or time, or clothes or food. They were such compelling pictures, even when people are familiar with the broader refugee story."[6]

Similarly, the Migrant Offshore Aid Station (MOAS), whose rescue boats in the Mediterranean had saved more than 10,000 lives, saw a fifteen-fold increase in donations in just 24 hours. It was reported that over two thousand people pledged £150,000, compared to a previous record of £10,000. In many cases, people were voicing frustration with their government's lackluster response to the plight of refugees and migrants. "People are saying they don't want to be bystanders any more," MOAS's director Martin Xuereb told the *Guardian*. "We are increasingly understanding that behind every statistic, every number, there is a life – a life who has a mother, a father or a sibling, a grandparent."[7]

The Swedish Red Cross, which had just recently set up a fund specifically for Syrian refugees, reported the "mean number of daily donations during the week after publication of the photo was more than a hundred-fold greater compared with the week before,"[8] an increase that continued at that level for five weeks after the photo was published. World leaders publicly reacted in dismay, contacted each other, and during Canada's federal election, the photographs ignited a contentious debate over the country's response, given that the Kurdi family had wanted to join relatives there. Liberal party leader Justin Trudeau, who would become prime minister, reiterated his party's pledge to allow 25,000 Syrian refugees to enter the country.

The photograph, it seemed, could be about us as well as the other; the firewall between people had been allowed to dissolve, at least momentarily. But given the current media climate, with masses of images competing against the perspective of any single photograph, many of them manipulated or simulated, this may be the last iconic photograph to activate such a widespread and constructive response to a tragedy. (The photograph of the attempted assassination of Donald Trump, his fist raised with the American flag behind him, is iconic but in a different way. It represents what critics such as Jean Baudrillard called the "hyperreal," appearing to be more real than reality itself in a mediasphere that is increasingly self-referential, simulating rather than exploring the larger world.)

Instead, we can now imagine other images, including those generated by artificial intelligence, serving to inflame enmities and deepen already widening societal fractures. On social media, these are the kinds of images that all too often attract large followings. Writing in *The Atlantic*, Charlie Warzel observed: "In 2014 – squarely in the halcyon days of social news – 75 percent of adults surveyed by Pew said that the internet and social media helped them feel more informed about national news. But by 2020, the conventional wisdom had shifted. That year, a Pew survey of more than 10,000 people found that 'US adults who mainly get their political news through social media tend to be less engaged with news and, notably, less knowledgeable about current events and politics.'"[9]

Simultaneously, in the United States, print magazine circulation has decreased by more than 50 percent since 2002, with a loss of nearly 2,900 newspapers and almost two-thirds, or 43,000, of its newspaper journalists since 2005, making it difficult to highlight a particular photograph for an extended time on a front page.[10] Now, according to another Pew Research Center survey, a large majority of U.S. adults (86 percent) say they often or sometimes get news from a smartphone, computer, or tablet, while 56 percent say they do so often, a trend away from

"Earthrise" commemorated on U.S. postage stamps, 1969.

print media that is similar to those in many other countries.[11] More disturbingly, a 2023 survey by Gallup and the Knight Foundation reported that half of Americans already "believe [that] national news organizations intend to mislead, misinform or persuade the public to adopt a particular point of view through their reporting."[12]

Previously, photographs could provide a shared focus on major events and help provoke social change. In 1968, for example, there were many such images: "Earthrise," astronaut William Anders's photograph of the earth seen from outer space made on Christmas Eve, 1968, showed the earth for the first time from outer space, vulnerable and alone in the vastness of the cosmos. The image helped kickstart a global environmental movement;

it was placed on postage stamps and, sixteen months later, the first Earth Day occurred, acknowledging the fragility of the planet and our responsibilities as caretakers. Others that year included the photograph of two Black athletes giving a Black Power salute on the medals stand at the Mexico City Olympics, each with one black-gloved fist raised in protest; Senator Robert F. Kennedy, forty-two years old, lying in a pool of blood in the kitchen of the Ambassador Hotel in Los Angeles after being fatally shot while campaigning for president, a busboy trying to comfort him; civil rights leaders pointing from the balcony of a Memphis motel towards the shooter who had assassinated Dr. Martin Luther King, Jr., when he was thirty-nine; student protesters in Mexico City and Paris in violent confrontations with the police; the summary execution on a Saigon street of a suspected member of the Viet Cong; emaciated, starving children in Biafra during the war; Czech citizens in Prague surrounding an invading Soviet tank, and many others.

Today there are few such credible markers. Viewers are left destabilized, unsure as to what to believe and unable to participate in the civic discourse that a democracy needs to sustain itself, leaving them with feelings of political powerlessness. A 2022 Pew survey found that only 38 percent of adults in the United States were following the news closely, whereas in 2016 there were 51 percent who did so.[13] Instead, many now fall back on their own beliefs, unwilling to be swayed by evidence to the contrary. And others simply deny the existence of troubling photos, as the ethos of contemporary entitlement, "the customer is always right," makes such denials acceptable.

The result is that societies, in their confusion, become increasingly vulnerable to autocrats. As Hannah Arendt asserted in *The Origins of Totalitarianism*, "If you want to destroy people's ability to resist control, you must destroy the distinction between truth and lies, because if you can't believe anything, you can't act."[14]

In the weeks following the start of the war between Gaza and Israel, the BBC published an article on two four-year-old boys, Omer and Omar, one Israeli and one Palestinian, who were killed in the early days of the conflict. Their deaths became the subjects of a social-media battle, with some people arguing online that it was not Omar who was depicted, but a doll; others, that Omer and his sisters did not die but are "crisis actors," people paid to perform a tragedy. Omar's mother, who confirmed to journalists that her son had been killed by an air strike, was forced to protect her child's memory from this grotesque accusation: "They have no right to say he is a doll." And a friend of Omer's family, all five of whom were reportedly massacred, said, "To deal with their death is hard enough, and all these comments make it even worse."[15]

Previously, rather than being belittled, photographs of children brutalized by the actions of adults could become iconic, serving as pleas for the violence to stop and for societies to advance. Such was the case with the horrific photos of fourteen-year-old Emmett Till, an African American child beaten and lynched in 1955 by racists in Mississippi. When his mother decided to allow pictures of young Emmett's body to be shared with the press, public reaction to the images helped to spark the Civil Rights movement.

Similarly, in 1976 photographer Sam Nzima took an apartheid-era photograph of twelve-year-old Hector Pieterson, his lifeless body in the arms of an older child, his sister walking next to them, after he was killed by security forces during a schoolchildren's peaceful demonstration against the teaching of Afrikaans as the primary language of instruction. According to Nzima, the photograph caused Nelson Mandela to remark, while unveiling a memorial for the child, "When we saw this picture, we said enough is enough."[16] Nzima himself, warned of the government's intention to retaliate against him, had to go into hiding and give up his career as a photographer.

Vietnamese photographer Nick Ut's iconic image of nine-year-old Kim Phuc, her body burning from the napalm that had been

Photograph by Sam Nzima of Hector Pieterson
being carried, *The World*, June 16, 1976.

dropped from a South Vietnamese plane in 1972, was equally powerful. It had to withstand attempts to discredit it. President Nixon privately wondered if the photograph was staged, saying to his chief of staff, H. R. Haldeman, "I wonder if that was a fix," what would be called "fake news" today. However, the evidentiary weight of this photograph and others made that day could not be repudiated, and given photography's credibility at the time, Nixon was unable to dismiss the horror that it evoked, even as it stoked resistance to the war. "Napalm bothers people. You get a picture of a little girl with her clothes burnt off," Haldeman said. "I wondered about that," Nixon replied.[17] The brutal killing depicted in the image increased doubts and resistance to the war and one year later, newly re-elected president Richard Nixon directed his administration in a significant reduction of U.S. troops.

Ut was aware of the desire to discredit his image and, when contacted by CNN, said that General William Westmoreland, the U.S. military commander in South Vietnam, had questioned the photo, but AP and NBC both had photographs that showed planes dropping the napalm.[18] Westmoreland also alleged that the child had been burned in "a hibachi accident."[19] But the photographic evidence would prevail, and, pre-internet, there was no social media presence that could attempt to contest its claims.

A photograph like Ut's and those of others could also be seen as emblematic of much larger issues. James Nachtwey, a celebrated, veteran photographer who has covered many conflicts, commented, "There was more power and more truth in the pain and suffering of one nine-year-old girl than in all the political spin devised by America's 'best and brightest' to justify an unjust war."[20]

The ability of such imagery to provoke a meaningful response, educating people and provoking governments to act, was a major reason why so many photographers chose to cover such difficult situations. This impact was also part of an implicit contract that

they had with those they photographed to do more than portray
them in a violent, life-threatening situation, but to try and be
helpful as a witness.

In 1989, while I was lecturing in La Plata, Argentina, to about
fifty young South American photojournalists, a Chilean
photographer posed a pointed question: how could a photograph
be made that would change his government, then a dictatorship?
He had been inspired by the large-scale response that I described
to Eddie Adams's photograph of a member of the Viet Cong
being summarily executed on a Saigon street in 1968, shot in the
head by a police chief, which was published widely, including
on the front page of the *New York Times*. Five years later, a year
after Nick Ut's similarly disturbing photograph of Kim Phuc was
published, all the U.S. troops were withdrawn from Vietnam.
The consensus is that such imagery was able to provoke a
decisive shift in public opinion as many reconsidered their
support for the war.

Of course, there was never a guarantee that any individual
photograph would prompt such a massive reconsideration.
But in the case of the Vietnam War, these photographs could
be upsetting enough to deepen and intensify the widespread
doubts that already existed as to the conduct of the war. Adams,
for his part, was not trying to produce a photograph that would
become an anti-war symbol: he was prouder of "Boat of No
Smiles," his 1979 reportage on Vietnamese refugees fleeing in
boats, which was thought to have helped loosen U.S. immigration
laws for some 200,000 people who were being denied entry. He
felt that his more famous photograph oversimplified what had
happened – General Loan, who did the shooting, had just lost
his best friend and his family, massacred by the Viet Cong – and
he felt guilty that his photograph had helped to ruin the rest of
the general's life. "Two people died in that photograph," Adams
would write in *Time* years later. "The recipient of the bullet and
General Nguyen Ngoc Loan. The general killed the Viet Cong;
I killed the general with my camera."[21]

The impact of these and other photographs made during the
Vietnam War lingered and would concern those who assumed
power afterwards. Fifteen years later, during the first Persian
Gulf War, in an effort to avoid what President George H. W. Bush
called "another Vietnam," photographers were excluded from
the battlefield. They were replaced by televised simulations, with
various on-air consultants commenting on the war in ways that
made it seem virtual (*The Gulf War Did Not Take Place* was the
title of Jean Baudrillard's book published the following year), as
well as by images such as those shown from a camera mounted
on a "smart" bomb as it hurtled towards its target, a technology
employed to supersede the empathy of the photographers as well
as their readers who would otherwise have been witnessing war's
inevitable horror.

Photographs that directly addressed the physical consequences
of the conflict and might turn the public against it were negated
in an orchestrated "image war" that emerged. Pictures of an
American missile destroying a bunker in central Baghdad were
quickly obfuscated by a cloud of questions meant to nullify their
impact: Were the Iraqi dead civilians or soldiers? Who was at
fault? Was it all staged? As a 1991 front-page headline in the *Los
Angeles Times* proclaimed, "Images of Death Could Produce Tilt
to Baghdad."

As American troops were being welcomed home with a ticker-
tape parade viewed by millions (unlike after the Vietnam War
when returning soldiers were unrecognized and at times reviled),
I wrote in an Op-Ed for the *New York Times* that "In trying
to suppress images of civilian and military casualties, of war's
extraordinary and inescapable horror, the officials who allowed
only carefully restricted photo opportunities also obscured the
contributions of these soldiers on parade. Even they have few
images to remember their experience by." Photographers were
denied because "If one could not see as a smart bomb could –
anonymously, successfully – then seeing was thought to be too
dangerous."[22] The image war that was ignited then continues

today, including on social media, where it has become even more inflammatory.

While these restrictive policies were modified for the second Gulf War, there was still a strategy in place to mitigate any potential fallout: photographers were required to be "embedded" with troops and to sign contracts stipulating under what circumstances their images could be published. Even the flag-draped coffins containing the bodies of American soldiers returning home were temporarily placed off limits for them. Similarly, there was no iconic imagery to crystallize an understanding of the longest war in American history, the twenty-year war in Afghanistan, so that when the Biden administration pulled all American soldiers out, we understood little about why the war had been fought and the suffering that would result for those, particularly women, who remained after the sudden retreat. War is ugly and horrific, and the more it can be kept sanitized and distant the better it is for governments afraid of public dissent.

Much of the most riveting iconic imagery that has emerged in the 21st century has been made by the billions of non-professionals who outnumber the few paid journalists and are free of the formal constraints imposed when working for mainstream media. They can be spontaneous, raw, emotional, and very personal, given that much of what they depict may be of their own family, friends, and neighborhood.

These more fluid, participatory images coming from the non-professionals, rather than staking a claim to being definitive, use a visual language that tends to be more detail-oriented and quotidian, with few elaborately constructed attempts at large, authoritative statements and little interest in conforming to the repetitive archetypes that occur in the press. This collapse of the boundaries between author and reader, now that so many can have both roles, makes it possible for media to function in a more conversational manner, particularly given the omnipresence of cameras and the technology to distribute the photographs that result (an iPhone advertisement referred to "one billion roaming photojournalists").

Whereas a potentially iconic photograph might have difficulty overcoming today's widespread skepticism towards conventional media, corroborating networks of trust online can support such witnessing, including work by non-professionals. In 2004, for example, the most revealing photographs to emerge from the Iraq War were those made by the soldiers themselves, who were torturing Iraqis incarcerated at the Abu Ghraib prison. The whole world saw the hooded man, forced to stand on a box, with wires attached to his extremities. While the professionals had been muffled, their photographs too often simplifying what was happening in a World War II-style conflict depicted as between good and evil, the soldiers had used their own digital cameras to tell a much more compelling, raw, and horrific story,

ABOVE LEFT   A demonstration in front of the U.S. Supreme Court to oppose violations of international human rights by the United States at Abu Ghraib prison, February 9, 2005. Photograph by Larry Downing/Reuters.

ABOVE RIGHT   A hooded prisoner forced by U.S. military personnel to stand on a box while attached to wires at Abu Ghraib prison, Iraq, November 2003, photographed by a U.S. Army soldier. Pictorial Press Ltd/Alamy Stock Photo.

one in which they participated. Now if we want to know how a war is progressing, it may be the images on the soldiers' portable devices that will tell us in the most detail.

Other images kickstarted the role of the citizen journalist: photographs of the bombing of the London Underground in 2005, and of Neda Agha-Soltan at a 2009 protest in Tehran disputing the government's election results, looking into a bystander's cellphone as she lay dying on a street from a bullet shot into her heart (she would become *Time*'s "Person of the Year").

The social media photographs of the Arab Spring became a major form of resistance to dictatorships, including the 2011 image taken from a bystander's video of a woman being dragged and beaten by police in Egypt's Tahrir Square, her clothing ripped to expose her blue bra, making the subjugation of women explicit. Later, the 55,000 photographs that a military policeman code-named Caesar smuggled out of Syrian prisons in 2014 documented the execution of some 11,000 young men who were officially reported to have died of natural causes. That could have been enough to cause the world to intervene.[23] Alas, it did not, but the amateur video by a teenager documenting the 2020 murder of George Floyd by Minneapolis police did provoke national and worldwide protests and the eventual punishment of the police responsible. All these photographs and videos by non-professional photographers depicted events and underlined critical issues in vivid and compelling ways.

While people have begun making efforts to promulgate imagery like this more widely, it needs to be more systematically curated and made available, even when there is no outbreak of news. For example, high school students from schools worldwide could periodically select some two dozen images from their neighborhoods or cities, on their own or perhaps as part of a social studies class, explaining why certain photographs or videos are important in their context. Specialists could do more of the same on specific themes, choosing imagery from a variety of topics while explaining their importance, letting the reader know, for example, which of the myriad images produced by experts on climate change are the most significant for the future of the planet.

The first assignment I usually give to my students, who come from many different countries, is to curate the social media from their country of origin, to provide an insider's view. A Chinese student, for example, chose what seemed to be a rather banal photograph of middle-aged parents holding hands in the middle of the street. However, as he explained it, they were attempting to prevent the noise of traffic while their children took university entrance exams nearby. Several years ago, a student from Gaza showed photographs, not of the destroyed buildings we are used to seeing, but of the variegated, sophisticated cuisine that he presented as their own. Photographs like these can teach us, the general readers, much more than can be found solely in the news.

Today, it can be the photographers posting on social media who relate the agonies of the world in a much more visceral way, often relating their own personal experiences to contextualize what a viewer sees, including the vulnerability of his or her own family and friends. After a brief reunion with her children a week after the conflict began between Israel and Hamas, Samar Abu Elouf, a Palestinian photographer living in Gaza who has worked frequently for the mainstream press, confided, "I meet my children after a week of working as a photographer during the war. I was inspecting the bodies while taking pictures out of fear that they might be among them."[24] And on her Instagram account, along with photographs that she had made of children in Gaza, she asked a question similar to the one that the Chilean photographer had asked in Argentina: "Every morning, every evening, and every moment, I ask myself: What photo does the world want to see in order to stop this war? More than 8,000 Palestinian children from the Gaza Strip were killed in 75 days, and many of the children have become without parents, and a large number have lost their limbs, and the largest number are

displaced and displaced inside tents. In extreme cold, they die
of hunger. What do you want to see to move your feelings more
to save the remaining children alive???? They are just waiting
to be killed!!!" Her post, from December 20, 2023, received
thousands of likes.[25]

While many people who post imagery on social media provide
insider perspectives and expert insights that fill in gaps that
news organizations may overlook (some photographers in Gaza
have followings in the millions), their work may be difficult to
locate for those who are not already sufficiently motivated or
informed. And even as many people may prefer the first-person
approach to witnessing, others may be more comfortable with
publications that feature journalists with more reportorial
points of view.

And, of course, given that there are few barriers to publishing,
there are those on social media who have no commitment to
the common good, whose work may masquerade as journalism
but attempts to exploit and deepen fissures in societies,
frequently based upon faulty or fabricated evidence. As Vaibhav
Vats reported in *The Atlantic* from India: "A grim video of a
beheading by a Mexican drug cartel was shared as an attack on
Israeli citizens. A nine-year-old photograph of Israeli Prime
Minister Benjamin Netanyahu and his son, taken before the
latter departed for his military service, was portrayed as the
leader sending his offspring to war. Footage of a funeral staged
in Jordan to evade a pandemic lockdown was misrepresented as
Palestinians faking deaths in Gaza. A 2014 video of the Islamic
State destroying a mosque in Syria was labeled as the Israeli
bombing of a Palestinian mosque."

Why? Vats explains: "Dispensing with complexity and real-world
consequences, the disinformation machinery of the Hindu right
has been operating in an amoral zone, treating the Israel-Hamas
war as little more than an entertaining spectacle happening
somewhere far away, and as a windfall for its Islamophobic

agenda."[26] And, as often happens now, the accuracy of the imagery posted online is not an issue for those who are already convinced of the rightness of their own opinion.

Today there is an image war in which nearly anyone can participate, just as the role of the photograph in conventional media has been diminished by a generalized disbelief in its veracity. While photography could in the past rise above the ideological fray to assert the existence of certain events and situations, serving as a societal referent, now it is more easily discounted as biased and misinformed. Adding to the problem is the emergence of photorealistic AI-generated synthetic media, produced without the use of a camera, which serves to "poison the well," making people suspicious even of actual photographs and videos.

To illustrate the confusion, Adobe, the company leading the Content Authenticity Initiative – "a community of media and tech companies, NGOs, academics, and others working to promote adoption of an open industry standard for content authenticity and provenance"[27] of digital media that includes the BBC, AP, AFP, the *New York Times*, and many others – is also selling synthetic images generated by artificial intelligence of Gaza and Ukraine and other places, that publications can use to illustrate their articles; the people writing the prompts to create the images may never have visited the places depicted.

So, for example, Adobe Stock features synthetic images said to be of Ukraine, including one with an attractive young woman in the foreground, dressed in a sweater and scarf, smiling at the non-existent photographer with her hands raised. It is captioned as "An image of a street protest capturing the authentic emotions and expressions of individuals advocating for social change. Concept of genuine activism." It is labeled "Generated with AI," with the caution below it "Editorial use must not be misleading or deceptive." Another image is captioned "A dynamic shot of activists engaging in a sit-in protest, peacefully occupying public spaces to draw attention to their cause. Concept of non-violent direct action." This is a similar AI-generated image, but this time it is a young man with his arms raised in the center. Each of these images is among those that one can "Download free with trial." Their publication online, even if accompanied by the "Generated with AI" label, hardly promotes a more authentic understanding of current events.

Synthetic imagery can also be used for things that *should* have happened but did not. The Instagram account Happy Children of Palestine was created as a commentary on the difficulties many Palestinian children have endured even before the most recent war began, and it utilizes images generated by artificial intelligence of non-existent children smiling and laughing in a bakery, drinking water, or in a playground, arguing that this "artwork, though borne from artificial intelligence, reflects a harsh truth. A reminder that without peace, the playgrounds lie silent, the swings unmoving, and the hopeful eyes of the young are forced to witness scenes of a script written by the hands of conflict and adversity."

While AI-generated synthetic media is only beginning to proliferate online, its capabilities make people wary even of genuine imagery. As Hany Farid, a professor at the University of California, Berkeley, and a specialist in disinformation, told the *New York Times,* "The specter of deepfakes is much, much more significant now – it doesn't take tens of thousands, it just takes a few, and then you poison the well and everything becomes suspect."[28] That leads people to accuse media outlets and those in power, as the *Times* suggests, of "brazenly trying to manipulate public opinion by creating A.I. content, even when the content is almost certainly genuine."[29]

At the same time, conventional media outlets have been reluctant to explore issues in depth, in part due to limited budgets. Long-term assignments and the photo essays that result are more difficult to find. In 2023, Don McCullin, probably the

Jan Rose Kasmir confronts the U.S. National Guard outside the Pentagon during a 1967 anti-Vietnam War march that helped to turn public opinion against the war. Photograph by Marc Riboud, Washington, D.C., 1967.
© Marc Riboud/Fonds Marc Riboud au MNAAG/Magnum Photos

most respected war photographer in the late 20th century for his extensive coverage of conflicts in Biafra, Vietnam, Northern Ireland, and elsewhere, described the current situation: "Photojournalism is dead. We've become obsessed with glamour and gloss: footballers, narcissism and gossip. Nobody wants the pictures I used to take."[30]

Now photojournalists and videographers, limited in what they can cover by local or state authorities and lacking the necessary financial resources as media companies reduce staffs and assignments, may be thrown into situations without the ability to explore their context and ramifications, so that the photographs that result inevitably tend to reflect preconceptions instead of deeper realities. In addition, it's dangerous work, now that journalists and media professionals are often targeted

by warring parties and no longer protected by their status as
press. An unprecedented number have been killed covering
the Israel-Gaza war.

As a result of this changed media climate, representatives of
the foreign press may find their coverage challenged, judged by
insiders as uninformed and biased, and criticized by outsiders
as insufficiently supportive of their own points of view. But
without the larger overview previously offered by mainstream
media organizations, readers and viewers may be less likely to
encounter subjects that they might otherwise have overlooked.

And as the role of the photojournalist shrinks, many parts of the
world are left unexplored until breaking news erupts. There had
been little attempt, for example, to understand the daily lives of
Palestinians in Gaza before the violence and conflict that broke
out on October 7, 2023. Who are the teachers, the doctors, the
poets, the parents, and the children who live there? What are
their hopes and dreams? Without that kind of knowledge, it is
all too easy, for example, to regard all Gazans as monochromatic,
and that in turn makes it easier to foist false, invented narratives
on a public that has little information with which to counter
them.

Similarly, why have the ambitions of Jewish settlers on the West
Bank dominated the news over the years while the work of
Israeli peace activists, including some who were casualties of the
initial Hamas onslaught, has been largely unexplored? Are the
Israeli activists' goals any less valid? Or those of their Palestinian
counterparts? These individuals and groups do not serve to stoke
the media's fascination with the more spectacular manifestations
of violence; photographs of people meeting to resolve differences
are considerably less graphic. But without such context, conflicts
end up looking like indistinguishable variations of one another,
spectacles of violence and destruction, and as a result, the public
forum of ideas to which visual journalists could contribute lies
increasingly dormant.

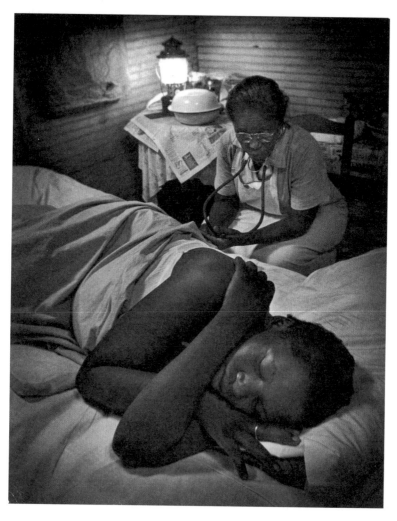

Midwife Maude Callen attending to a woman in labor in Pineville,
South Carolina, December 13, 1951. Photograph by W. Eugene Smith.
W Eugene Smith/The LIFE Picture Collection/Shutterstock

In the heyday of picture magazines, photo essays helped to transcend any such reactive coverage by exploring larger issues in more complex ways. In 1948 W. Eugene Smith, one of the preeminent essayists for *Life*, explored the somewhat lonely but heroic life of a country doctor in Colorado, and, over twenty years later, the destructive impact of mercury poisoning on the health of people in Minamata, Japan. His photographs of Maude Callen, published in 1951 as "Nurse Midwife," showed the dedication and hardship faced by the first licensed Black nurse-midwife in South Carolina. Affecting countless lives, she would deliver between six and eight hundred babies and train some four hundred midwives in her sixty-year career, providing at-home care in "an area of some 400 square miles veined with muddy roads" where white doctors would not go.[31]

Readers were so moved that the magazine could announce three weeks later: "Mail, money and gifts from readers in all 48 states have been pouring in to *Life* and to Maude Callen. So far, she has been sent a total of $3,689.03 plus a pair of rubber boots, a sewing machine, a portable incubator, a wrist watch and many boxes of clothing."[32] After receiving some $20,000 in donations, she had enough to build a clinic which, as Callen said in response, "isn't so big, but it looks like the Empire State Building to me."[33] Readers could be engaged, and people helped.

The positive changes that imagery like this help to provoke (Smith's work in Minamata also drew worldwide attention to the dangers of mercury poisoning leading to increased controls) have not been widely recognized. Over a period of four years, for example, South African-born photographer Gideon Mendel demonstrated the success of a pilot project that provided anti-retroviral medicines for HIV-positive South Africans. At that time, only 8 percent of Africans needing anti-retroviral (ARV) drugs were getting treatment, and Western governments and NGOs were reluctant to provide them, skeptical that Africans would be disciplined enough to take their medicines consistently.

Nomphilo Mazuza stands with her two sons Lindithemba, 10, and Pumlane, 8. Photograph by Gideon Mendel, 2006.

Responding to a question from me, Annemarie Hou of UNAIDS wrote, "I think it would not be too bold to say his work helped us reach 8 million people on treatment today." A similar project, "Access to Life," by eight photographers from Magnum Photos, working with the Global Fund to fight AIDS, Tuberculosis and Malaria, depicted people on treatment in nine countries; it resulted in $1 billion being raised for anti-retroviral drugs. The Japanese prime minister, after spending only forty-five minutes viewing the exhibition, reportedly doubled his country's contribution to $800 million.

Similarly, some years ago, I worked on a photographic campaign, "Chasing the Dream," that drew on imagery and texts from young people, as well as those made by the Argentinian photographer Diego Goldberg and the journalist Roberto Guareschi, to advance the UN's Millennium Development Goals, helping to ensure better education, healthcare, and environmental conditions for young people in economically underdeveloped countries. The exhibition, with photographs and short texts coming from youth in Brazil, Cambodia, India, Jamaica, Uganda, Morocco, the Kyangwali refugee settlement in North Uganda and Ukraine, was shown in the lobby of United Nations headquarters in New York in 2005, during a conference to mark the first five years of the campaign and to plan its future. Years later, I was surprised to read of a study demonstrating that, due to this fifteen-year campaign, "The upshot is that somewhere between 21–29 million more people are alive today than would have been the case if countries had continued their pre-MDG rates of progress."[34] While our exhibition was only a small part of the effort, it pointed to the ability of photographs to move people, including the hundreds at the opening presided over by then Secretary General Kofi Annan.

Don McCullin's photographs of brutality and starvation in Biafra in the 1960s are considered a turning point in the use of photographs by humanitarian organizations. His work attracted the attention of Bernard Kouchner, a founder of Doctors

Without Borders, the Nobel Prize-winning organization that was established after Kouchner and others went to Biafra to see for themselves the suffering there. According to Kouchner, it was McCullin's imagery that "marked the start of a collaboration between press and medics, without which humanitarian efforts are doomed to fail."[35]

While it is the graphic imagery of disaster that is usually considered newsworthy, the solutions that photographs may help to provoke, bettering the lives of millions, are often overlooked. This resource, if lost, will marginalize already vulnerable populations, making their situations even less visible and interventions less likely.

Meanwhile, the photograph is already diminished in its ability to provoke discussions that may lead to helpful responses. In the U.S., for example, there has been considerable and passionate debate about using photographs to document the grisly aftermath of gun violence in schools. After gunmen with military-grade assault rifles killed nineteen students and two teachers in a Uvalde, Texas, elementary school in 2022, many clamored for the release of the photographs of the children's pulverized bodies, arguing that this would bring society to its senses and lead to more rational gun laws.

Almost two decades after a mass shooting at Columbine High School left twelve teenagers and a teacher dead in 1999, the students there wanted to make sure that if they too were killed by gun violence, the pictures of their dead bodies would be circulated widely. Citing the impact of previous iconic photographs, they expressed the hope that their deaths would not be in vain. They asked other students to join them in a campaign called My Last Shot, in which a sticker was attached to each student's identity card or cellphone, reading: "In the event that I die from gun violence please publicize the photo of my death. #MyLastShot."[36]

"We've become numb to the stats. Orlando 49, Vegas 59, Parkland 17 – numbers that lack humanity," the Columbine students' website stated. "And progress isn't made through censorship. It's made when we see humanity at its worst, and together, bring out our best. Because in order to find a solution, we have to see the problem. Even if it's hard to face." Infuriated by "a world where post-shooting photos are mothers hugging their daughters, and police tape," these teenagers campaigned for a potential photography, an empty frame that may one day need to be filled because too few adults were willing to act to prevent such calamities in the future. A belief in photography's power to advance social justice lingers among this younger generation, aware, and even envious, of the legacy of a socially conscious photography to help propel such change.

In 2019, the group's seventeen-year-old founder, Kaylee Tyner, explained that she saw these photographs traveling primarily through social media. "Our lives are centered around social media and, contrary to popular belief, it is actually a lot more helpful than a lot of people think," with social media "mak[ing] it more personal," constructing narratives different from those that appear in the conventional media. Tyner experienced this when she stumbled across a video of the Parkland school shooting that "a kid had just taken inside the classroom as the room was being shot up." She explains, "I could just hear other kids screaming and seeing all of it in the video. And it was like, *That was their reality.*"

It's a reality that she and others, like Peter Bouckaert, who distributed the photograph of Alan Kurdi, wish that more people, including those in power, would confront and use for change. "If you're uncomfortable with them releasing a video," Tyner said, "you should be uncomfortable with the fact that their school was shot up." Tyner's mother Andrea said that, when she first heard about the My Last Shot campaign from Kaylee, it took her breath away. "The thought made me so uncomfortable," she said, "but I know it's more of a vehicle for awareness." As Kaylee stated: "The ultimate goal is for these images to never come out."

If such images did eventually come out due to another tragedy, however, they might not have the desired effect. As the critic Neil Postman pointed out, comparing Aldous Huxley's *Brave New World* with George Orwell's *1984*: "Orwell feared those who would deprive us of information. Huxley feared those who would give us so much that we would be reduced to passivity and egoism."[37] Adding the graphic imagery of the casualties of school shootings to the media ecosphere could add to the "passivity and egoism" that Huxley described, as well as to the surfeit of horror that is endlessly promoted online. It would also lead to more traumatization of parents and children, not only those who had suffered directly in Uvalde, and the photographs could be used by some to advocate for more guns in the hands of schoolteachers and others. And some, as we are now seeing in relation to the war between Israel and Gaza, would probably argue that these photographs, like those of Omer and Omar, were fabricated as part of a plot against gun owners.

In today's world, having photographs of one's brutalized children circulate on social media allows others to recontextualize them, even "like" or "dislike" them online, depriving these children's families of the space and peace necessary to mourn them. As Nelba Márquez-Greene, whose daughter Ana Grace was killed in a school shooting nearly a decade previously, eloquently wrote in a *New York Times* article: "After the Uvalde [Texas] shooting, my inbox was flooded with requests from allies and advocates for autopsy photos of my daughter. What did they think a photo could do that the truth of the tragedy had not already conveyed? Do we really expect the same legislators who watched the storming of the Capitol on Jan. 6 and met it with tepid rebuke to somehow be moved by images of my murdered child or those of other parents?" Her conclusion: "Our country's problems with guns will not be fixed with images of dead children."[38]

To protect the families who must identify the dead children, authorities often decide to use DNA testing rather than showing them the photographs, in order to spare them the sight of the destroyed bodies of their loved ones. The public can imagine such atrocities without photographs, and their absence should not prevent others from finding the personal and political will to respond. As Márquez-Greene suggests, writing about her own devastating loss: "Lower your gaze and do the work without asking for any more blood from me."

Some potential subjects have learned to resist the media's tendency to emphasize violence and favor demeaning caricatures. The Twitter campaign #IfTheyGunnedMeDown emerged after the fatal 2014 police shooting of unarmed eighteen-year-old Michael Brown in Ferguson, Missouri. It was designed to help young African Americans draw attention to the tendency of media outlets to use racist stereotypes when describing Black people who are killed in similar circumstances. They shared the images of themselves that they thought such outlets would use – and juxtaposed them with more everyday photographs, such as of them performing in a high school band or graduating, that they hoped would be used to represent them if they were gunned down. It is no wonder that many prefer social media to represent themselves.

Issa Touma, a Syrian gallery owner and photographer, used a similar approach in a book project titled *Women We Have Not Lost Yet*.[39] Published in Arabic and English in 2015, the collection recounts the tenuous lives of young women gathered in his Aleppo gallery during a ferocious week-long attack on the city. In the images, their faces are printed in two parts on separate pages, without their eyes being shown. "The women we are seeing in these photographs are still alive," Touma writes. "They are not different from any woman in the West." In the text that accompanies one portrait, twenty-one-year-old Dima explains, "Since the war started, I've said goodbye to so many people. I stopped meeting people so I wouldn't have to say goodbye any

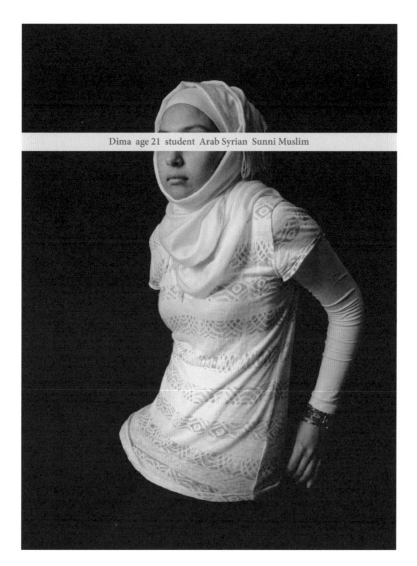

Dima age 21 student Arab Syrian Sunni Muslim

"Dima, Age: 21, Occupation: Student, Nationality: Arab Syrian, Religion: Sunni Muslim." From Issa Touma, *Women We Have Not Lost Yet*, 2018.

more. I've lost any sense of being alive. I'm staying in Aleppo to finish my studies, and every night I count the bombs exploding around my house until I fall asleep."

For professionals, the transition to digital platforms has made many new strategies possible along with older ones. They can now work with multiple media; link with other projects; engage the reader interactively; collaborate closely with the people being photographed; use non-linear as well as linear narratives; photograph proactively; increase context for each photograph; be more present personally; and explore solutions rather than focusing only on disaster. And, given the changes in the way photographs are understood, they can move into realms that are more conceptual, abandoning some of the emphasis on symptoms to explore the underlying problems that have caused them. In attempting to visualize the future impact of current policies, they may even find themselves one day able to employ artificial intelligence while being transparent as to its use.

In a media revolution, reinvention is necessary, particularly given the urgent challenges emerging worldwide to which photographers were previously able to respond with considerable impact. Otherwise, it will no longer be photography's unbearable relevance that will be celebrated, but its increasing irrelevance that will be mourned.

Chapter Five

Expanding
the Frame

"The most alarming photograph of
climate change today."

"The photograph offers
irrefutable evidence that
this man, this horse and this
bridle existed. Yet it tells us
nothing of the significance
of their existence."

John Berger, *Another Way of Telling*, 1982

In 2007, the prestigious Musée de l'Elysée in Lausanne staged a prescient exhibition, "We Are All Photographers Now!" Anyone could send in photographs and have them projected on the walls of the museum along with recognized artists, making the contemporary democratization of the medium explicit.

In the years since, the digital revolution has provoked an extraordinary profusion of imagery online but a striking paucity of strategies to explore the world in more nuanced, coherent and impactful ways. The cornucopia of images, buoyed by numerous "likes" and links, dwarfs the contributions of professionals who remain mostly faithful to a more measured style that still tends to lean on photography's faltering reputation as authoritative.

Susan Sontag anticipated how this could happen. In her 2003 book *Regarding the Pain of Others*, she observed: "Photography is the only major art in which professional training and years of experience do not confer an insuperable advantage over the untrained and inexperienced – this for many reasons, among them the large role that chance (or luck) plays in the taking of pictures, and the bias toward the spontaneous, the rough, the imperfect." She did not anticipate, of course, that there would be such an enormity of images that the impact of any single one would be fleeting, if it had any impact at all, or that software would emerge to homogenize "the spontaneous, the rough, the imperfect," according to the current camera manufacturer's take on consumer entitlement.

The 1930s had seen a transformation in photography, as the introduction of portable cameras and more light-sensitive films led to an increasingly close-up, visceral photography, one that was buoyed by the emergence of picture magazines such as *Vu*, *Picture Post* and *Life*, eager to take advantage of this new sense of authenticity. Then, the camera's reportorial capacities prompted such awe that a static Robert Capa Spanish Civil War photograph of soldiers casually seated under an overhanging rock for protection was titled, by England's *Picture Post*, "In the Heart

of the Battle: The Most Amazing War Picture Ever Taken." The
rather breathless caption began, "This is not practice. This is
war," and continued, "These men crouching beneath the ledge
feel the shock of every shell-burst. They know that a better aim
will bring their own piece of rock down on top of them. They
know that in a minute's time they may be ordered forward over
the shell-swept ground. They are not worrying. This is war, and
they are used to it."[1]

Photographers were able to publish a series of photographs as
an essay or story with an accompanying headline, article and
captions, to have their images juxtaposed against each other in
diverse ways to amplify their meanings, to command the public's
focus with graphic front pages, and, not least, to expect to be
paid for their work. In 1947, the Magnum Photos cooperative
of photographers was founded, advocating a new model, later
adopted by many others, in which the photographers would
keep the copyright to their own photographs, even if produced
on assignment, and then the agency could re-sell their members'
work to publications in other countries. In the era of print
publications, this was feasible. As a result, photographers could
afford to work on long-term projects of their own choice.

Now, unlike in the 1930s, an increasing flexibility in making
photographs whenever and wherever one wants has produced
considerably more dissonance and much less clarity of focus.
Not only is everyone now a photographer, but also a potential
publisher, often without any explicit commitment to editorial
standards. And, on cellphones, the limited space to present
photographs that are properly sequenced and contextualized
can make each single image seem that much more deracinated
and inconsequential.

In a *New York Times* piece entitled "When Everyone Becomes
a War Photographer," critic Jason Farago reacted to the imagery
emerging around the large-scale violence between Hamas and
Israel: "In Syria, in Ukraine and now in Israel and Gaza, war

in the 21st century has become a fire hose of digital imagery
– a perpetual torrent of jerky and pixelated images, often from
amateurs, frequently of uncertain source, that looks nothing like
the high-resolution war-as-spectacle that media scholars foresaw
during the Persian Gulf war of 1991. On our small screens we are
now closer to war than ever before. We are farther than ever from
making sense of it."[2]

Online media may be weaponized, saturated with conflict-
related imagery, some of it fabricated or appropriated, that may
verge on the voyeurism of a snuff film as various parties strive
to outdo the other's grisly sensationalism. Previously, editors
would take care that much of the most gruesome imagery would
remain unpublished, in part not to revictimize those in distress,
but also to avoid alienating readers and, of course, advertisers,
as well as the children who might be accidentally exposed to
the trauma depicted. Viewed as little more than hosts of online
platforms, social media companies are rarely held accountable
for what appears online and frequently promote inflammatory
and inaccurate depictions to increase their audiences.

However, the digital environment does provide serious
photographers with a variety of opportunities, including new
ways of distributing their work, which can make it possible
to reach large audiences while circumventing editorial filters
that may have restricted their input, particularly that which is
first-person and experiential. Nevertheless, social media, for all
the freedom that it allows, may attract only a limited audience
composed primarily of those who are already in agreement with
a particular point of view, anticipating that their expectations
will be largely confirmed. For example, a student of mine,
Jesse Kornbluth, recounted in class how he had pointed out
the existence of fake imagery on both a pro-Palestinian and a
pro-Israel site, one an AI image and the other a staged video.
The reactions were similar, as hundreds of viewers responded,
many contending that these inaccuracies were unimportant
since they already knew the truth of what was going on.

The digital environment also allows for other ways to produce and present work, some of them responding to photography's transforming status. The great promise of digital interactivity enables various forms of collaboration; photographers can invite the perspectives of insiders and outsiders, specialists and non-specialists, engaging with both the past and the present, to explore the multiple meanings of the photographs that result. They can add links, responses, rollovers, crowd-sourcing, discussion groups, and other strategies to deepen and dispute their own perspectives. They can supply additional context, particularly on websites, and choose to employ non-linear narratives to further engage readers, making them more explicitly co-authors who must choose their own pathways to explore. And, with just a click, the online environment offers resources that, for the first time, allow for a photograph's meanings to be buttressed with information from multiple other sources.

Departing from Capa's oft-repeated maxim, "If your pictures aren't good enough, you aren't close enough," distance can now be considered a more credible way of exploring the systems that underlie the symptoms that traditionally have been photographed. One can ask, for example, why Capa's seated soldiers were at war, investigating the societal reasons (increased economic disparities due to the Great Depression, labor unrest, the power of the Catholic Church, etc.) and also exploring who these soldiers were when not in uniform. In a multimedia environment, the voices of those whom one photographs can be included, speaking not only about themselves but about larger issues, as can links to work by others with both insider and outsider perspectives.

In a quest for greater authenticity, photographers can also make their work more personal, describing what occurred outside the frame of the photograph as well as their own feelings in experiencing a situation or event. They can make their own codes of ethics available to the reader, who just needs to click on their name, making it clear whether or not they refrain from manipulating their photographs with software, as well as

establishing their commitment to other standards as both an
eyewitness and human being.

The non-linear narrative possibilities of the digital, as well
as its ephemeral nature, make it an inviting environment for
approaches that are less intent on making realities concrete
and more focused on investigating complexities, particularly
given our increased awareness of photography as both subjective
and interpretive.

A growing number of photographers are experimenting
online, in exhibitions, and in the thousands of photobooks
published annually, with a variety of strategies. Many of these
are dialectical and conceptual, attempting to interrogate rather
than certify, preferring key questions over assertions, looking
away from the center of action to discover the telling details
that intimate larger issues, and acknowledging multiple voices,
including their own, eager to invite those depicted to collaborate
on their own representations.

That which lies outside the frame, both spatially and temporally,
becomes as important as the image within if one tries to
address, as Berger put it, "the significance of their existence."
The fractional second in which the shutter is released is a barely
sufficient starting point. As I wrote in *In Our Time: The World
as Seen by Magnum Photographers* (a collection of photographs
representing forty years of global history): "The film records
during such small bits of time that this book's four hundred
pictures, representing over four decades of work, were most
probably taken in a total of some four seconds – one second,
more or less, per decade."[3]

The search for more expansive ways of exploring societal issues
has been growing over decades. Philip Jones Griffiths's 1971
volume, *Vietnam Inc.*, produced after two-and-a-half years of
photographing in the field, presents some of the expected images
of heroism in war.[4] But they are powerfully undermined by

critical juxtapositions of photographs and frequently sardonic captions. (Griffiths photographed, wrote, and designed the book, which he had originally titled, *WHAM VIETNAM* – the first word an acronym for the U.S. officials' slogan, "winning hearts and minds.") For example, one caption above a double-page photograph of soldiers dismounting from a helicopter in the brush reads: "U.S. combat troops arrive, outnumbering the enemy 3 to 1 and possessing the most sophisticated military hardware; the job seemed easy. Earlier, spirits were high among the troops, intoxicated as much by the spectacle of their own strength as by the cold beer delivered to them daily."

Another double-page spread shows a command center with soldiers looking at computer printouts, the caption reading, "The computer that 'proves' the war is being won. Data collected for the 'Hamlet Evaluation System' is analyzed by it to 'see who loves us.' Optimistic results on the 'my-wife-is-not-trying-to-poison-me-therefore-she-loves-me' pattern are reliably produced each and every month." The 1966 discussion by a pilot commenting on napalm is gruesome: "We sure are pleased with those backroom boys at Dow. The original product wasn't so hot – if the gooks were quick they could scrape it off. So the boys started adding polystyrene – now it sticks like shit to a blanket. But if the gooks jumped under water it stopped burning, so they started adding Willie Peter (WP – white phosphorus) so's to make it burn better. And just one drop is enough, it'll keep on burning right down to the bone so they die anyway from phosphorus poisoning."

He focused also on the impact of the American presence on Vietnamese women, who "sit outside American bases waiting to enter to serve the soldiers as everything from laundry maid to prostitute." He includes a close-up photograph of a woman being assaulted by U.S. navy personnel after dancing for their colleagues, as well as a section on young girls who sell "girlie paintings" to the soldiers and end up in the sex trade that emerged in response to their presence. Another image shows soldiers looking at a brochure for the car that they might buy when returning stateside: "Car purchasing during combat. Salesmen used to follow GIs into the field to make a sale 'so that the boys will have a real reason for wanting to get home in one piece.' Today they find it safer to have the GI choose his car's trim and upholstery by mail order."

Accompanying photographs taken on an aircraft carrier he wrote, "The sailors and pilots on board have never been to Vietnam. They have never seen the faces of their victims, the Vietnamese people." Later in the book, Griffiths offered a rare juxtaposition of an image of an American pilot, one of those who might have been responsible for dropping bombs, with a badly burned man. He also placed a full-page photograph of a woman in a field, mourning over the grave of her dead son, alongside one of the commander of an American unit who, Griffiths writes, carried around a skull at his farewell party. By controlling layouts in this way, he was able to suggest cause and effect, a way to understand the origins of the widespread suffering he witnessed and to delineate the profoundly divergent realities that people experienced.

Vietnam Inc., as its title implies, contextualizes the war as a form of corporate takeover rather than a battle for democracy. It employs a strategy similar to Ernst Friedrich's 1924 *War against War!*, a vituperative, multi-lingual condemnation of World War I and the culture from which it emanated. Friedrich featured children's toys extolling battle, made differences of class explicit, and displayed numerous photographs depicting the dreadfully disfigured faces of soldiers. It was an attempt, sadly unsuccessful, to use photographic witnessing to end the abomination of war for all time.

Photographic history is replete with books portraying war, condemning its horrors but also at times underlining it as spectacle. When photographer Tim Page, who was injured in action four times, was asked to do a book that was intended to take some of the glamor out of war, he was incredulous: "Jesus,

Philip Jones Griffiths, *Vietnam Inc.*, 1971.
© Philip Jones Griffiths/Magnum Photos.

FIRST SPREAD "PACIFICATION, alias "Rural Reconstruction," or "Revolutionary
Development," or "WHAM" ("winning hearts and minds"), is Americanization.
Inside the briefing room at the MACV headquarters in Saigon, which is where
officers have the validity of their own perspectives reinforced."

SECOND SPREAD "U.S. COMBAT TROOPS ARRIVE, outnumbering the enemy
3 to 1 and possessing the most sophisticated military hardware; the job seemed
easy. Earlier, spirits were high among the troops, intoxicated as much by the
spectacle of their own strength as by the cold beer delivered to them daily."

PACIFICATION, (a.k.a. "Rural Reconstruction," or "Revolutionary Development," or "WHAM" ("winning hearts and minds"), is Americanization. ...briefing room at the MACV headquarters in Saigon, which is where officers have the validity of their own perspectives reinforced.

U.S. COMBAT TROOPS ARRIVE, outnumbering the enemy 3 to 1 and possessing the most sophisticated military hardware, the job seemed easy... ...garbo, spirits were high among the troops, intoxicated as much by the spectacle of their own strength as by the cold beer delivered to them daily.

take the glamour out of war? How the hell can you do that?
You can't take the glamour out of a tank burning or a helicopter
blowing up. It's like trying to take the glamour out of sex. War
is good for you..."[5] He spent fourteen years in recovery after a
piece of shrapnel destroyed a golf-ball-sized part of his brain.

Photography can also at times be used more proactively in
pursuit of peace, particularly if one is willing to forego the
spectacle. In 1996, after the Dayton Peace Accords ended a
vicious four-year conflict in Bosnia among Serbs, Croats, and
Muslims, I approached Kevin McKenna, the editor of the
newly created *New York Times on the Web*, arguing that since
the Web was a new medium only in its infancy we could use
it in less conventional ways. Instead of adding to the many
graphic depictions of violence, we could focus on its possible
resolution. The *Times* agreed, and photographer Gilles Peress,
who had previously covered the war extensively, returned to
Bosnia for six weeks on assignment to explore the possibilities
of peace with a non-linear project in mind.

"Bosnia: Uncertain Paths to Peace" was published online
for three months in the summer of 1996.[6] It was an attempt
to engage in a more complex and substantive exploration
than would typically appear in print (an eight-page photo
essay by Peress would also be published in the *New York
Times Magazine*). We intended, rather than imitating a print-
based essay, to take advantage of strategies made possible by
the Web, such as non-linear narratives, discussion groups,
contextualizing information, including an array of maps and a
chronology of events preceding the recent violence, panoramic
imaging, the photographer's reflective voice, an active
engagement of the reader, and the addition of video. Unlike
the analog photograph, the digital image could also serve as a
node to be linked elsewhere.

From the beginning, it was clear that the photographer needed
to be closely involved in the creation of such a project, rather

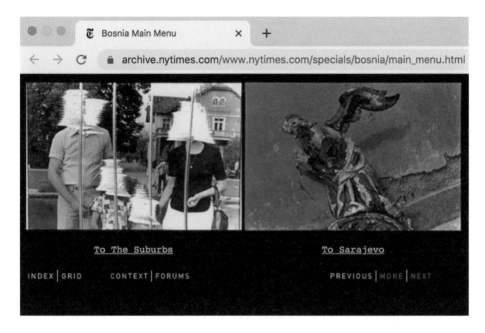

"Bosnia: Uncertain Paths to Peace." Photographs by Gilles Peress,
the *New York Times on the Web*, 1996. © Gilles Peress/Magnum Photos.

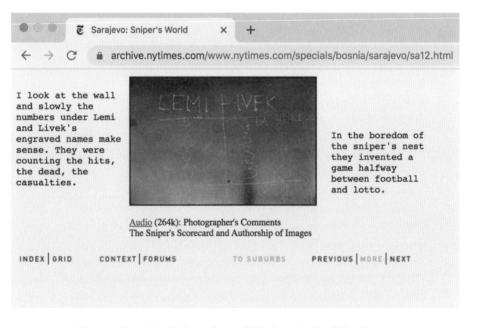

"Bosnia: Uncertain Paths to Peace." Photographs by Gilles Peress,
the *New York Times on the Web*, 1996. © Gilles Peress/Magnum Photos.

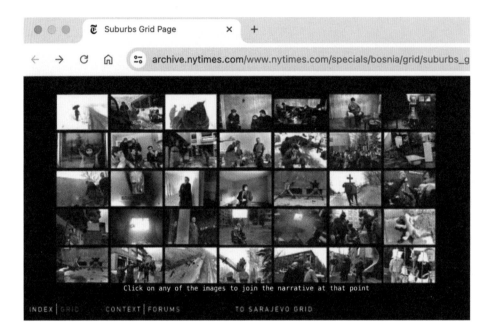

"Bosnia: Uncertain Paths to Peace." Photographs by Gilles Peress,
the *New York Times on the Web*, 1996. © Gilles Peress/Magnum Photos.

than simply handing over the imagery to others for selection,
as often happens in print media. As the project's editor, I could
not simply select the "best" images and string them together,
regretting that other strong photographs had to be excluded due
to a lack of space. In this case, the space was nearly unlimited,
and the photographer needed to articulate his understanding of
each photograph to help us understand and make linkages that
would permit overlapping narratives to reflect the complexities
of a society attempting to transit from war to peace.

As the eyewitness, aware of what was inside and outside each
frame, both spatially and temporally, the photographer also had
a pivotal role after the actual photography was accomplished,
narrating the various situations he encountered and creating
connections among them (while in Bosnia, he would send back
rolls of film from which I would select frames and discuss with
him the pictures he had not yet seen over the telephone). It

would take several hours for a viewer to go through the finished site, given its many pathways and contextualizing information; since it was a non-linear hypertext, each reader could approach it differently. Peress later remarked that the process of creating the website seemed the equivalent of making three books or one feature film.

I learned, as the editor, to interrogate every image for possible meanings, given that each image could be linked to others. In doing so I grew more sharply aware of my own distance from the events and people being depicted, and more motivated to understand them as individuals rather than as emblematic of certain roles. With all the non-linear, contextualizing, multimedia possibilities of the Web, generic imagery of a grieving mother, wounded combatant or traumatized child seemed a crude and unnecessary shorthand. Instead of propelling the narrative, they limited it, invoking the usual tropes.

The meanings of the Bosnia photographs were often unclear. While the photographer was still in Sarajevo, I selected from uncaptioned contact sheets a photograph of a man lying dead on the ground. It turned out, surprisingly, that he was an actor playing dead; a feature film on the siege of Sarajevo had begun production only four days after the shelling had stopped. I came to realize that it was possible to either collapse each photograph's potential meanings with a defining caption or sustain the ambiguities in the photography to provoke new thinking, not only about what each image depicted, but about the future of Bosnia, a country only recently at peace.

Twenty-seven years later, in *Peace, Complexity, Visuality*, a book published in 2023, researchers Rasmus Bellmer and Frank Möller found the "Bosnia: Uncertain Paths to Peace" project's embrace of ambiguity essential, including for the pursuit of peace that required what they call a "tolerance of ambiguity." "One of the most common approaches to visual images (save for images of art)," they wrote, "is disambiguation, i.e., establishing the meaning of a given image, exploring how this meaning has come into being, and analyzing how the image and the meaning assigned to it operate in and on society (discourse analysis posing as visual analysis). In contrast, we suggest acknowledging and capitalizing on the plurality of meanings that all images necessarily carry with them and, by so doing, learning to cope with ambiguities beyond visuality as well. Thus, we treat images' non-coherence as a merit rather than a liability that has to be replaced by visual consistency."[7] They argued that this tolerance of ambiguity is necessary for keeping an open mind while navigating the societal complexities that must be considered in the making of peace.

Previous commentators had grasped other implications. In *Print*, Darcy DiNucci wrote: "Clumsy as today's low-bandwidth presentations must be in some particulars, the site indeed pioneers a new form of journalism. Visitors cannot simply sit and let the news wash over them; instead, they are challenged to find the path that engages them, look deeper into its context, and formulate and articulate a response. The real story becomes a conversation, in which the author/photographer is simply the most prominent participant."[8] Joe Goia, writing in the online journal *Salon*, cited "the McLuhanesque consequences of photography freed from the confines of material reproduction." He added, referring to the relative insubstantiality of screen-based photographs: "They seem barely more permanent than the moments they presume to record. Quick to load, the photos present themselves with the ease and weight of dreams." Rather than conveying a Newtonian sense of cause and effect, this new form of imagery was more quantum-like, concerned with potentialities, including those that might lead to peace.

Peress and I worked with some 400 small photos on the walls of his loft, with differently colored lines connecting the various images, playing a kind of four-dimensional chess as we pondered how to structure the photo essay. If the reader clicks on this image near the window, where would it take him or her? To the image on the other side of the room? What if a reader clicked on the image but only on the person on the left; where would it lead? Why would a reader want to become involved in such a new form of reading? How interactive could (and should) the experience be? When would we lose a reader's interest? When would this become gimmicky, a kind of game that would demean the experience of those in the pictures?

We decided that the metaphor of the journalist should be the strategy for navigating the essay. Just like a journalist who arrives at the Sarajevo airport not knowing where to go or what specific story to explore, the reader would be required to click on images without knowing where they might lead. Unlike with a book or magazine, you could not flip forward to assess what was coming. Each click of the cursor would put a reader on a new screen with differing perspectives and unknown possibilities, while two screens, each with uncaptioned small photographs organized in grids – one compiled from the screens concerning Sarajevo and the other from those dealing with the surrounding suburbs – would allow a reader to reject a linear approach by clicking on any of the photographs to link to some other part of the reportage. Whatever confusion resulted for the reader seemed minor compared to the distress and chaos in Bosnia at that time.

We paired Peress's photographs with his own written text and recorded voice to allow his emotional reactions and philosophical questions to contextualize the imagery, extending their implications beyond the reach of typical identifying captions. For example, on arriving in Sarajevo, Peress added this narrative to his aerial photographs: "Flying above the land frozen and virgined by the snows, I start to see the scars, the trenches, rows of homes, suburbs of a better life, wrecked by house-to-house combat, by front lines through living rooms, gardens, turned into mine fields. From this vantage point, embracing the totality of destruction, silenced by the winter air, we drift upon the city: Sarajevo." Or, accompanying pictures of the snipers' lairs: "The sniper's world is a cubist virtual reality where both killer and victim have mapped out space in a game of life and death, and where ten centimeters of unthought potential are met by the crack of the gun. When the sniper is 'on,' the air vibrates, the sound of a shot can come at any time, and the street changes its form from a positive space to a negative one, more defined by its outlines than by its center. And now that war is gone, you can visit the other side of the mirror from which he was looking at you."

The idea was to challenge previous limitations of storytelling without alienating the reader who, coming from the analog world, still had little idea that photographs online could be clicked on (we added instructions). The essay opened with an uncaptioned photograph that was, in fact, a re-photographed snapshot of a Muslim family in which the face of each family member had been erased by a drill bit; the disfigured snapshot was all that was left when this family returned home after four years. Then readers had to choose, clicking on one of two photographs that would take them either to Sarajevo or to its suburbs, unsure of what each choice entailed. And rather than publish conventionally violent photographs of war, we chose photographs that would help people understand the problems of reconciliation as well as its potentials, while providing forums for readers to discuss possible paths to peace (although some of what emerged was a vociferous articulation of their deep-seated hatreds).

Certain hopes for the project were not realized. I had wanted to engage the viewer's history of choices, via clicks, as a primary navigational determinant, so that if a reader clicked on several pictures showing the Muslim community, he or she might later be surprised to be prohibited from selecting pictures of Serbs (the computer might temporarily freeze, for example). This could remind the viewer of what had happened to inhabitants of Sarajevo who might have been assaulted or murdered not only over their own ethnicity, but also because of their previous choice of friends and neighbors.

Peress, freshly returned from a variety of experiences, was given center stage as an author. As a result, rather than relying on the authority of the *Times*, by constructing the site to encourage an open-ended conversation among the photographer, the people living in Bosnia, and the reader, we could be seen as undermining the authority of the newspaper. This explains, in part, the reaction when in 1997 the *Times* nominated the project for a Pulitzer Prize in public service. The Pulitzer committee immediately rejected it for not having been printed on paper; the more ephemeral, open-ended, collaborative experience it offered seemed to have contravened the mission of the serious, authoritative journalist. No longer was the continuum from subject to reporter to editor to reader conceived as if in a straight line; the Web allowed for, and promoted, a more collaborative, zigzag approach, as well as the opportunity for doubts and uncertainty. It was a far cry from the *Times*'s slogan, "All the news that's fit to print."

Certainly, the Bosnia story benefited from the support of a major newspaper, as well as from its creation before the explosion of social media with its billions of competing, disposable images. It was produced nearly from scratch in an era before templates began to dictate the presentation of media online and made it harder to create idiosyncratic narratives based upon unique designs. When I later returned to the *Times* to do two smaller online projects involving individual photographers, I was told by the staff that I would no longer be able to ask the reader to scroll horizontally – a survey had shown that they preferred only vertical scrolling.

The relationships among author, subject, and reader have evolved as photographers have pursued their own trajectories in storytelling. In another project, "Rich and Poor," published in book form over a decade earlier in 1985, Jim Goldberg photographed wealthy and poor people in San Francisco, who were asked to comment on how they were portrayed, in their own handwriting. Their notes are often revealing: next to one

WE LOOK LiKE ordiNAry PEOPLE!

WE have a Terrible LifE

EMily. S.

My wife is Acceptable.
Our relationship is satisfactory.
                    Edgar G.

Edgar looks splendid here. His power and
strength of character come through. He is a
very private person who is not demonstrative
of his affection; that has never made me
unhappy. I accept him as he is.
     We are totally devoted to each other.
                              Regina Goldstine
Dear Jim:
     May you be as lucky in marriage!

From Jim Goldberg, *Rich and Poor*, 1985. Jim Goldberg/Magnum Photos.

portrait of an older couple, the wife, Regina Goldstine, writes in a refined script: "Edgar looks splendid here. His power and strength of character come through. He is a very private person who is not demonstrative of his affection; that has never made me unhappy. I accept him as he is. We are very devoted to each other." She ends by addressing the photographer with her wish: "May you be as lucky in marriage!" Her husband, on the other hand, is rather more phlegmatic: "My wife is acceptable. Our relationship is satisfactory." In contrast, above and under another image, a portrait of a woman in an apartment holding a small girl, Emily S. writes: "We look like ordinary people! We have a terrible life."[9]

Today, it's much easier to use this collaborative approach on digital media. For several years I have been asking my students to make "interactive portraits" in which the voices of the people portrayed can be recorded as they comment on to what extent the portrait shown on the camera's screen represents them. One no longer "takes" a photograph but *makes* one, in collaboration.

So, for example, Ashima Yadava asked the man she photographed, looking serious and dignified, wearing glasses, a tie, white shirt and jacket, whether the photo she made represents him. His response: "No, because I'm a smiling person. I actually like to be smiling, you know. I do that just about most of the day." She then asks: "So if you're not smiling, it's not you?" He answers: "Yes it's me but...in that picture I...don't think it really tells me because it more looks like I'm sad or something like that."

Becca Screnock made a close-up portrait of a young man dressed casually, his sunglasses perched on his head, and asks him, "Do you think this a photo that depicts you...that says who you are?" He answers, "No." "Why not?" His answer: "Because I don't think any picture ever will." "Why?" His answer is surprising: "Because it's just, I don't know, you can't see inside a person in a picture. You can see parts of them that leak through, but that's just a glimpse."

From "Whale Hunt," Jonathan Harris, 2007.

Zahra Mirmalek photographed an unhoused man at night on
a New York City street, looking cold, scruffy, and under-dressed.
His comments erase any stereotype: "This picture is definitely
not me. I used to be much more clean-cut, a much better-looking
person. I'm very very depressed and sad about the way I look
right now as a human being. But, you know, with an opiate
addiction and being homeless on the streets in the freezing
cold winter it's really hard to maintain yourself, let alone shave,
shower, or anything like that on the streets of New York City."

Under a portrait, rollovers can also be used to reveal additional
photographs of the same person if the photographer wishes,
allowing the viewer to discover an image that may amplify or
contradict the first. The unhoused person can be shown as
he was in his former abode, with a job; the man who thinks of
himself as smiling can contribute a second image from his family
album. It is a simple strategy, even though it is rarely used, and
one that enhances the portrait's authenticity and complexity
while resisting the sway of one single depiction. It is also one

that is much more difficult to accomplish in print, where
concealing images under others is usually not feasible.

Another former student, Cristóbal Olivares, used the idea of
interactive portraits to portray some of the 460 demonstrators
in Chile who, while protesting against economic conditions, had
lost an eye or had one eye badly damaged when security forces
shot at their faces with rubber bullets and tear gas guns. He asked
them to comment on how they now appear. One forty-six-year-
old man said, "I look at the mirror and I look at my own self now
and I say 'I am mutilated'"; he hopes that with a prosthesis he
will look normal again. The destructive impact is made personal,
intimate, and long lasting, not just a dry statistic from an event
relegated to the past.[10]

Some photographers are, literally, exposing more of themselves
by giving a greater role to their own corporeal beings, making
their subjectivity explicit. Jonathan Harris, in his 2007 project
"Whale Hunt,"[11] linked his photography to his own biological
responses to what he was seeing while allowing viewers to
intervene in different ways. He set out to document a remote
region of northernmost Alaska "with a plodding sequence of 3,214
photographs, beginning with the taxi ride to Newark airport,
and ending with the butchering of the second whale, seven days
later. The photographs were taken at five-minute intervals, even
while sleeping (using a chronometer), establishing a constant
'photographic heartbeat'. In moments of high adrenaline, this
photographic heartbeat would quicken (to a maximum rate of
37 pictures in five minutes while the first whale was being cut
up), mimicking the changing pace of my own heartbeat."

One of the purposes of this project, as he explained it, was
"to experiment with a new interface for human storytelling"
so that the "full sequence of images is represented as a medical
heartbeat graph along the bottom edge of the screen, its
magnitude at each point indicating the photographic frequency
(and thus the level of excitement) at that moment in time.

"Paragraphica," Bjørn Karmann, 2023. Courtesy Bjørn Karmann.

A series of filters can be used to restrict this heartbeat timeline, isolating the many sub-stories occurring within the larger narrative (the story of blood, the story of the captain, the story of the Arctic Ocean, etc.). Each viewer will experience the whale hunt narrative differently, and not necessarily in a linear fashion, constructing his or her own understanding of the experience." Harris, both programmer and artist, states that he was also trying to establish empathy with the computer by subjecting himself "to the same sort of incessant automated data collection process that I usually write computer programs to conduct." Unfortunately, due to the retirement of Adobe Flash Player in 2020, the interactive interface is no longer accessible online; this is a recurring problem as software evolves.

The potential for linking photography to biological functions such as heart rate, blood pressure, and brain waves is exciting as a way of connecting with the photographer's thoughts and emotions, but also potentially problematic. Imagine, for example, in a more dystopian universe attaching a camera capable of identifying its subjects to someone considered by society to be, for one reason or another, deviant, and then punishing the person if they are caught looking for a length of time at the wrong person or thing, particularly with a speeded-up pulse rate.

Recently, researchers using artificial intelligence have been able to measure the brainwaves of a person looking at a particular image and then largely recreate that image. "Meta has developed an artificially intelligent (AI) system that can scan a human brain and quickly replicate the images that a person is thinking about – in a matter of milliseconds," *PetaPixel* reported.[12] The potential for people unable to speak is exciting, but as the technology develops, the privacy of thoughts may be at risk. Wim Wenders 1991 film, *Until the End of the World*, features a similar technique for the sharing of brainwaves, which is used by the character played by William Hurt to communicate to his blind mother (Jeanne Moreau), so that she can see her relatives; the aboriginal people working at the Australian lab flee the project, alarmed by the invasion into people's minds.

Cameras can be linked to other systems that circumvent or amplify the photographer's vision. In 2023, for example, Danish designer Bjørn Karmann invented a "camera" without a lens that he calls Paragraphica.[13] It uses location data along with artificial intelligence to generate synthetic images of the place where the apparatus is located. Rather than an image, the viewfinder provides at first a real-time description of its current location using text, including time of day, address, weather, temperature, date (including if it's a specific holiday), and nearby points of interest. There are three controls: the first controls the radius of the area in which the camera searches for data (Karmann compares this to setting the focal length in an optical lens); the second creates certain amounts of visual noise, comparable here to the grain in film; and the third determines how closely the resulting image should follow the instructions in the initial paragraph that was generated. Comparing it to a traditional camera, Karmann explains, "the higher the value, the 'sharper,' and the lower, the 'blurrier' the photo, thus representing focus." The device can also be used online.

If such data-driven "cameras" were made with the intention of allowing a viewer to meander through history, seeing the same street at different periods, such as before and after gentrification, before and after flooding, before and after rioting, and so on, it might radically enlarge the idea of the present to include the past. Using artificial intelligence, we might also see synthetic images of one street decades into the future as it might be affected by urban renewal or by climate change, and that in turn could trigger a proactive response to limit or even avoid unwelcome developments. A pivotal constraint, of course, will be the limitations of the available datasets that may contain a great deal of imagery concerning well-documented peoples and places, but have much less to offer about other cultures and regions of the world; depictions of their histories would then inevitably become more speculative.

This "historical camera" approach diverges radically from the immediacy associated with the "decisive moment," which was Henri Cartier-Bresson's philosophy of photography as "the simultaneous recognition, in a fraction of a second, of the significance of an event as well as of a precise organization of forms which gave that event its proper expression."[14] With this technology, moments are part of a larger flow, while history is not only of the past but shapes the present which, in turn, affects the future.

Other boundaries once thought to be impermeable are being crossed. Now companies are beginning to advertise systems that facilitate ongoing conversations with loved ones after their deaths. Developed from extensive interviews, photos and videos, these systems ensure that the survivor is, in a sense, never left behind. Thousands of people have already made files that others can converse with after their deaths, including the actor Ed Asner, whose son Matt "was blown away by it." As he told the *New York Times*, "It was unbelievable to me about how I could have this interaction with my father that was relevant and meaningful, and it was his personality. This man that I really missed, my best friend, was there."[15] But when he played it at his father's memorial service, some were moved, while others felt uncomfortable.

Ethical issues abound. Did the person who died give permission to be activated as a conversant, and with whom? Do these virtual dialogues make it harder for survivors to handle and resolve their grief? How accurate can such a conversation be, and can the advice it gives to a loved one be harmful, given the occasional tendency of artificial intelligence systems to "hallucinate" and go off the rails? These virtual resurrections can also cause significant problems if deceased performers are made to star in new movies or sing new songs, as a recent strike in Hollywood made clear.

The musician Brian Eno long ago foresaw certain of these possibilities, asserting in the previously mentioned 1995 interview in *Wired*: "In the future, you won't buy artists' works; you'll buy software that makes original pieces of 'their' works, or that recreates their way of looking at things. You could buy a Shostakovich box, or you could buy a Brahms box. You might want some Shostakovich slow-movement-like music to be generated. So then you use that box. Or you could buy a Brian Eno box. So then I would need to put in this box a device that represents my taste for choosing pieces."[16]

•

As is often the case, the future has been percolating around us for some time now. "What served in the place of the photograph, before the camera's invention?" the English critic John Berger asked in 1980. "The expected answer is the engraving, the drawing, the painting. The more revealing answer might be: memory."[17]

Considered less subjective and more reliable than memory, photography went on to displace it. It could certify the reality of the past while creating its own narrative to which personal remembrances became secondary. Did grandma wear pearls to her wedding? How many people attended a presidential inauguration? The answers could be found in photographs and that evidence was, until recently, difficult to challenge.

Now, however, as the photograph's status has been destabilized, its connection with memory has weakened in favor of what one wished to have happened. Magic Editor, the software from Google Photos, is described as "a new experimental editing experience... that uses generative AI to help you easily make complex edits and bring your photos in line with how you remember a moment."[18] Rather than being a "home for all your photos and videos," Google Photos is now "home for all your memories," the first time the company had changed its slogan in its eight years of existence.

Photography, it seems, was too harsh an arbiter. Now, grandma may have worn diamonds in one rendering of her wedding and no jewelry at all in another; we may no longer be sure from the visual evidence who she married, or if she married at all. Meanwhile, the audience at the inauguration may have been so massive that it dwarfed all previous ones; one can imagine a politician tasking an assistant to make that seem to have happened.

Of course, photography was never the sole arbiter of what occurred even though it often appeared to be. Each image needed to be contextualized to be understood, just as in a courtroom someone who was familiar with what was being depicted could be called upon to authenticate its essence. The photograph itself was a marker, a reference point, but not the whole story.

Many of today's photographers working on issues of memory and loss have understood the need for context and, just as important, for keeping contemporary events from disappearing into the past. In Argentina, with its tragic history of dictatorship and the torture and killing of many of its citizens, photographers have found innovative ways to transcend some of photography's limitations. For example, in his 2007 project "Ausencias" (Absences), Gustavo Germano re-photographed people in the locations where they had been photographed with family members decades earlier – although now these people have significantly aged, and in each photograph there is at least one person missing. The paired photographs evoke the lives never lived of those who had been "disappeared," beside the lives of those who have had no choice but to grow older bereft of their loved ones. The loss is doubled, and the past continues, harshly, into the present. These photographs were selected to be exhibited at the United Nations when the Mothers of the Plaza de Mayo spoke about their long campaign to hold the government accountable.

Also in Argentina, and using software not to erase the past but to make its impact explicit, Lucila Quieto's "Arqueología de la

An image of veteran James Sullivan is projected onto the home of his son, Tom Sullivan, left, as he looks out a window with brother Joseph Sullivan in South Hadley, Mass., May 4, 2020. Sullivan, a U.S. Army World War II veteran and resident of the Soldiers' Home in Holyoke, Mass., died from COVID-19 four days shy of his 100th birthday. Photograph by David Goldman, 2020. Associated Press/Alamy Stock Photo.

ausencia" (Archaeology of absence, 1999–2001) consists of
a series of constructed photographs in which adult children
of the disappeared were invited to create a new photographic
portrait with their missing parents. In this case, the transparent
use of software could be somewhat healing.

In a project in the United States, rather than photographing
former soldiers as they lay sick and dying from COVID,
Associated Press photographer David Goldman memorialized
them publicly, showing them as they had been, young and
vital in uniform.[19] He projected photographs of some of the
more than sixty people who died from COVID at the Holyoke
Soldiers' Home in Massachusetts onto the homes of their loved
ones at night, as their spouses, siblings and children looked out
from doors and windows, making private mourning visible at a
time when people had to isolate at home. Anecdotes about the
deceased appeared alongside the photos, and a reader could
hear the voices of family members telling stories. Alfred Healy,
91, for example, "loved corny jokes and adored his family. He
listened to audiobooks constantly and closely followed the news.
He devoured history and was quick with facts on U.S. presidents.
He was humble. He won a Bronze Star, but his family only found
out how decorated a soldier he was when he was gone. He was
a longtime U.S. Postal Service employee who rose to become
a town postmaster. He was sharp as a tack and liked to deem
things 'snazzy' or 'classy.' On his last night, the nurses gave him
chocolate ice cream and showed him photos of some young
relatives. And by dawn, he was gone."

The past was made to meld with the present, and the private
was situated so that the public could participate. Rather than
focusing on the tragic circumstances of their deaths, the
photographs projected were designed to honor those who died
and make the void caused by their loss all the more palpable.

In another evocation of memory and loss, several photographers,
including Celia A. Shapiro and James Reynolds, undertook

projects re-creating the last meals of inmates in the United States on death row as a way of drawing attention to the prisoners' social backgrounds, personalities, and their executions. Reynolds's series "Last Suppers," from 2009, contains a photograph of an unpitted olive on a plastic tray, with the explanation: "Victor Feguer asked for an unpitted olive because he thought it might grow into an olive tree from inside him. It was supposed to be [a] symbol of peace."[20] The text for Shapiro's photo essay, published in *Mother Jones* in 2004, begins: "When Arkansas executed Rickey Ray Rector back when Bill Clinton was governor, the mentally impaired inmate famously set aside half of his last meal – a pecan pie – for after the execution."[21] Viewers are drawn in to imagine what they might order as a last meal, recognize the banality of the choices available, and accept the meal's finality.

In a devastating twist to that portentous moment, Amnesty International used Reynolds' work and then, along with a photograph of the person, informed the reader that several years later further investigation showed that they should have been allowed to live. For example, "Cameron Todd Willingham asked for tater tots, ribs, enchiladas, onion rings, and two slices of pie for his last meal," the reader is told, a reconstruction of the meal presented. Then, with a photograph of Willingham with his laughing son on his shoulders, it is revealed that he was "executed in 1997 and presumed innocent in 2010."[22] More than desolate memorials, those final meals become symbols of deep flaws in a system meant to ensure justice.

Some of the most horrific photographs of atrocities ever taken are those of World War II Nazi concentration camps. When they were published after the war, many were shocked by their depictions of emaciated and dying people as well as those who guarded and tortured them, along with the masses of corpses and piles of eyeglasses and shoes. Susan Sontag famously remarked, "One's first encounter with the photographic inventory of ultimate horror is a kind of revelation, the prototypically modern revelation: a negative epiphany. For me, it was photographs of

Bergen-Belsen and Dachau, which I came across by chance in
a bookstore in Santa Monica in July 1945. Nothing I have seen
– in photographs or real life – ever cut me as sharply, deeply,
instantaneously. Indeed, it seems plausible to me to divide my
life into two parts, before I saw those photographs (I was twelve)
and after, though it was several years before I understood fully
what they were about."[23]

Many of these images of the Holocaust were made for
bureaucratic purposes, to be recorded for Nazi archives, not to
arouse the viewer's empathy. They became part of a methodical
attempt at genocide with the Orwellian label of the Final
Solution. First published in 1960 in German as *Der gelbe Stern*,
and later in several languages (in English as *The Yellow Star*,
the identifying badge that Nazis forced Jews to wear), Gerhard
Schoenberner's book of nearly two hundred images contained
many such forensic-style photos from German sources, as well
as a variety of textual materials from archives seized at the end
of World War II.

The book shocked many Germans with its clinical renditions
of mass killings and other atrocities, accompanied by excerpts
from documents that included field reports from SS officers and
concentration camp directors. In the abstract introducing his
article "Pictures of Atrocity: Public Discussions of *Der gelbe Stern*
in Early 1960s West Germany,"[24] Robert Sackett remarks that these
images became part of what historian Habbo Knoch called "the
return of the pictures," referring to the atrocity photographs that
the Allies had forced Germans to look at right after the war's end.

West German newspapers and magazines reviewed the book
overwhelmingly favorably, Sackett reports, with a "consensus
that its pictures would stir viewers emotionally and lead them
to 'the truth' about the Third Reich and its crime against the
Jews." He added that "there was also an appreciation of the role
of pictures in conveying historical understanding and, it was
hoped, in educating West German youth."

While certain kinds of horrors were not shown, Sackett's description of what the book contained is chilling. Readers "will see a human brain exposed by 'surgery' at Dachau, scalp and skull cut away (p. 158), will see photos of women awaiting their murder naked, forced to undress at the shooting site (pp. 96–97), or will see children, the elderly – face after face – in scenes of abuse." He argues that it was risky for the book's author to present these images for publication: "an extreme wager on his and his viewers' ability to overturn the intention for which these pictures were taken and replace it with compassion."

The photographs did, finally, provoke disgust and horror, indicting the executioners, even if after the fact, and enlarging the historical record. But they emerged in an era when the photograph was still thought to record essential truths, and to do it with extraordinary detail: "a picture is worth a thousand words."

Like all photographs they were made in a specific moment to be seen eventually as the past. And as the reader's knowledge of the larger context in which they were made begins to fade over time, the significance of the events that they depicted can become sidelined. As John Berger suggested, "All photographs are of the past, yet in them, an instant of the past is arrested so that, unlike a lived past, it can never lead to the present. Every photograph presents us with two messages: a message concerning the event photographed and another concerning a shock of discontinuity."[25]

Part of the shock is what Berger calls the "abyss" separating the time when the photograph was recorded from the moment when we view it, and the diminished meaning that may result. Another aspect can be the relative powerlessness of viewers to respond to the events depicted. The photograph, then, can serve to help establish a trace of events in memory but also to detach those traces, similar to Plato's concept of writing as a means of forgetting. Berger argues in *About Looking*, "The camera relieves us of the burden of memory. It surveys us like God, and it surveys for us. Yet no other god has been so cynical, for the camera

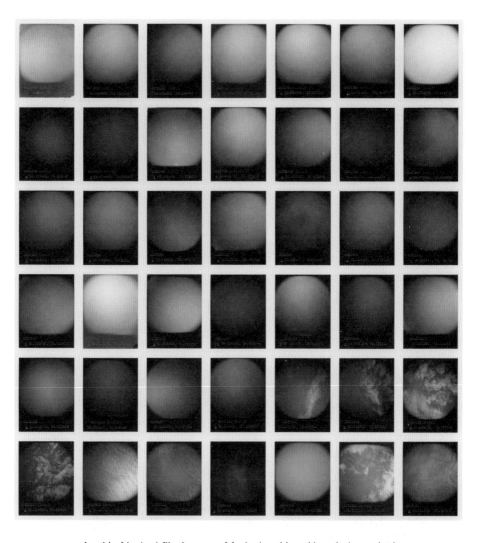

A grid of instant film images of forty-two blue skies photographed
with a Polaroid camera at every last known location of the
Auschwitz concentration camp and sub-camp system. Each image
is blind-stamped with GPS coordinates of the sky and the number
of victims beneath it. The Blue Skies Project by Anton Kusters.

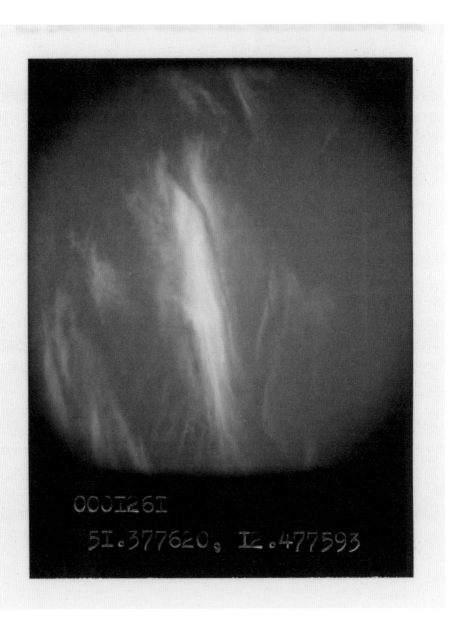

The skies over the Toucha concentration camp.
Photograph by Anton Kusters, The Blue Skies Project.

records in order to forget."[26] Referencing Sontag, Berger suggests
that this god is "the god of monopoly capitalism."

Interestingly, it was the 1978 four-part, nine-and-a-half-hour
American miniseries "Holocaust", a televised docudrama mixing
fact and fiction, that reintroduced the horrors of the Holocaust
to the general public and brought them newly alive for many West
Germans. Centered on the wartime experiences of two German
families, one Jewish and one Christian, it attracted some 50
percent of West Germans when it was aired in early 1979. After
each episode, historians answered some of the thousands of
questions phoned in by distraught citizens asking how all of this
could have happened. The acting of Meryl Streep, James Woods,
Michael Moriarty and others in this semi-fictional drama placed
the historical record into a national conversation. Subsequently,
"Holocaust" was named the German Word of the Year.

Not all responses were positive. As a survivor, the novelist Elie
Wiesel was outraged by the broadcast, writing in the *New York
Times*, "The witness feels here duty-bound to declare: what you
have seen on the screen is not what happened there. You may
think you know now how the victims lived and died, but you
do not. Auschwitz cannot be explained nor can it be visualized.
Whether culmination or aberration of history, the Holocaust
transcends history. Everything about it inspires fear and leads to
despair: the dead are in possession of a secret that we, the living,
are neither worthy of nor capable of recovering."[27]

Many now consider that photographs of the Holocaust, which
once served as powerful testimony, tend to banalize what
happened: a few are shown so often to illustrate the horrors
of the camps that they lose their specificity. Some people argue
for their removal from wide circulation to help them retain a
unique, sacred status, but in the era of easy digital reproduction
this may be an impossible task. Instead, it may be necessary
to investigate other ways of retaining their power. As Marian
Turski, the president of the International Auschwitz Committee

who himself survived the camp and the 1944 death march,
said in response to an exhibition by Gerhard Richter based
upon the only photographs made by prisoners at the Birkenau
death camp, "The part nobody who wasn't there can imagine
is the dehumanisation. I don't think naturalist painting makes
a sufficient impression to tell the story about the Shoah. To
me they are like documentation, like photographs, which were
forbidden in the camp. The only art which came close was not
realistic, but conceptual, where we are forced to think."[28]

Anton Kusters, a Belgian photographer, had a similar
perspective. He recently chose to photograph 1078 blue skies
over 1078 World War II concentration camps. To make them, he
"traveled 177,828 km, 95 percent alone, to every corner of the
former Third Reich"[29] over five-and-a-half years. He researched
the existence of the 1078 former official Nazi Germany SS
concentration camps, including 110 early camps first established
by local authorities as well as the six mass extermination
camps that were built later, based upon information gathered
in the United States Holocaust Memorial Museum seven-part
Encyclopedia of Camps and Ghettos 1933–1945.

Kusters employed a geo-positioning device to locate the sites
and weather apps to find out when the skies over them would
be blue. In an age of billions of uploaded images, he limited
himself to making three peel-apart Polaroid images of each
largely cloudless sky, the camera always set at the same exposure
to uniformly record the reflected light. A manual typewriter
stamped each 8 x 10 cm image with both its GPS coordinates and
the number of victims estimated at each location.

Kusters knows that, unlike digital files, one day these film-and-
paper images will fade away. He is not unhappy about that and
aware that photographing the past can be paradoxical. "There
was nothing left to see at over half of the places," he says, and
many of those living in the vicinity were unaware of the camp's
previous existence. "Often I was hopeless along the way."[30]

His collaborator, the musician Ruben Samama, used the same data as Kusters to create a sound piece lasting 4,432 days, the amount of time that passed from the establishment of the first concentration camp in 1933 to the closing of the last one in 1945. His piece generates an individual tone for each victim in the 1078 camps over a dozen years, the pitch changing according to the camp in which each person was held, forcing the viewer to confront time's passing and the eventual death of millions. Created with the software program Excel, widely used by businesses to calculate profits and losses, Kuster's piece in its architecture mimics the bureaucratic, systematic executions of Jews, gays, Romas, political dissidents, the physically and mentally disabled, prisoners of war, and others, during the Holocaust.

When Samama's sound piece was played several years ago at a conference lasting several hours in a New York museum, by the time the discussion ended, an enormous number of people had died in the parallel universe of the Holocaust created by this installation; an exact count of the victims was displayed. After listening, one has only to turn on the news to realize the horrors that arise and persist with us today – refugees in boats, Uighur Muslims in massive Chinese detention camps, Ukrainians under siege, Palestinians and Israelis in conflict, and the many more whose suffering is largely unrecognized.

The seemingly discordant existence of a blue sky can serve as a reproach. After the September 11, 2001, attacks on New York, Christopher Bergland wrote in *Psychology Today*. "My favorite tile for years was a simple blue tile with two small silhouettes of the Twin Towers in black with the words, 'THE SKY WAS SO BLUE...'" Newspapers at the time also similarly referred to "a crystal blue bowl of morning sky" (*Hartford Courant*), or "the kind of bright blue sky that people who love New York love best in New York" (*New York Times*), to describe what seemed at first to be a serene, beautiful day. "It was not just blue, it was a light, crystalline blue, cheerful and invigorating," George McKenna wrote in *The Puritan Origins of American Patriotism*. The canopy of the blue sky seems at the very least incongruous, as if heaven and hell should not be able to co-exist in the same frame.

Sometimes a blue sky can represent the last fragment of hope. When an older woman from Homs, a Syrian city that had been incinerated by war, described her home to a group of other refugees, "she paused for a moment, held her arms aloft as she looked at the ceiling," Coco McCabe wrote on OXFAM's website, "and managed just one sentence before sobs of longing shook her to her core, 'The sky is so blue,' she said."

The German novelist W. G. Sebald, as Mark O'Connell wrote in *The New Yorker* on the tenth anniversary of Sebald's death, also felt that "the recent history of his country could not be written about directly, could not be approached head-on, as it were, because the enormity of its horrors paralyzed our ability to think about them morally and rationally. These horrors had to be approached obliquely."[31] As a result, O'Connell asserts, "the writing itself gives the impression of being only the faint, flickering shadow of its actual referent. What Sebald seems to be writing about, in other words, is frequently not what he wants us to be thinking about."

It is as if Sebald wanted to consciously put us within Plato's *Allegory of the Cave*, where images flicker, tenuously connected to actualities. Sebald himself made photos with a small camera and visited flea markets to collect photographs, postcards, and other visual ephemera, which he sprinkled within his novels. There, they were used in dialogue with the text to further narratives that appeared both to be affirmed by these documents and called into question. What the uncaptioned photos depict is often unclear.

For Sebald, these photographs can serve a palliative function. In one of his novels, *Austerlitz*, the eponymous central character, himself of uncertain origin, "is always taking photographs and he entrusts his collection," Rick Poynor writes in *Design Observer*, "which 'one day would be all that was left of his life', to the

narrator, who uses them to assemble his story. After Austerlitz
has a breakdown, some of his photographs play a therapeutic
role, helping him to reconstruct his 'buried experiences.'"[32]

The perceived authenticity of a photograph can have a
therapeutic effect on people who, due to trauma, have lost access
to certain memories. For example, the book *Riley and His Story*
is a 2009 collaboration between a medic who served in the
U.S. military in Iraq's Abu Ghraib prison, with Monica Haller,
a college friend who helped him put together a book of his own
photographs and text. She subsequently collaborated on some
fifty books with other veterans, family members, and civilians.

"Many events in my time in Iraq were too complex, too horrific,
or beyond my understanding," Riley writes. "There were simply
too many things I witnessed there on a given day to process,
so I stored them as photos to figure out later. Pictures create
a concrete reality. At least I know these things happened. They
continue to serve that purpose." Haller describes the volume
they produced together as not actually a book but, using a
military term, "an object of deployment." It is also, she writes
on the book's all-type cover, "an invitation, a container for
unstable images, a model for further action. Here is a formula:
Riley and his story. Me and my outrage. You and us." In the
attempt to restore memories lost to war, the photographs and
accompanying text become an accusation.

Indirectly, Sebald's novels also probe large-scale societal ruptures
through parallel universes. His discussion in *Rings of Saturn* of
a film about silk cultivation in Germany early in the Third Reich
is "not so much a way of understanding the Holocaust, so much
as it is a way of making us think about how we can't understand
the Holocaust," O'Connell points out in *The New Yorker*. "We
see the hatching, the feeding of the ravenous caterpillars, the
cleaning out of the frames, the spinning of the silken thread, and
finally the killing, accomplished in this case not by putting the
cocoons out in the sun or a hot oven, as was often the practice

in the past, but by suspending them over a boiling cauldron. The cocoons, spread out on shallow baskets, have to be kept in the rising steam for upwards of three hours, and when a batch is done, it is the next one's turn, and so on until the entire killing business is completed."[33] This description of slave labor and mass extermination indirectly evokes the barbarities of the Holocaust, without serving either as explication or metaphor.

With his 1078 Polaroid photographs of recent blue skies, Kusters also depicts a universe parallel to the horrific past below. As the images and their metrics advance within the book, every page is calibrated to represent ten days between 1933–45. These blue skies do no more to explicate the vicious horrors of the Holocaust than did the sky that Wiesel remarked upon when deported to Auschwitz with his family at the age of fifteen. "Never shall I forget that night, the first night in camp," wrote Wiesel, "which has turned my life into one long night. Never shall I forget that smoke. Never shall I forget the little faces of the children, whose bodies I saw turned into wreaths of smoke beneath a silent blue sky."[34]

Kusters tells us one story while asking us to imagine another. His pictures ask how these skies could appear so tranquil after being a ceiling for genocide, and, in turn, how could we not reflect upon similar horrors that continue to exist under similar skies? And, in posing these questions, Kusters challenges the paradigm of the 20th-century photograph. He argues for it to be amplified, going beyond the direct recording of events to grapple with the unfathomable cataclysms of recent times, particularly in the current era that is enmeshed in the vertigo of "post-truth," when photographs are no longer seen as a reliable arbiter of events, able to provide trustworthy descriptions of the physical world that can provoke empathy and engagement with the issues.

Last century, the photograph confronted the public with evidence that was difficult to refute, and by doing so, challenged the morality of wars, highlighted the failures of civil rights

protections, and provoked a profound concern for the
environment. Kusters' photographs work differently, resonating
symbolically with what, as was mentioned earlier, Alfred
Stieglitz called "Equivalents," his description of his own abstract
photographs of cloud formations he made early in the last century.

Stieglitz meant his images to be viewed as formal expressions
that elicit emotional responses rather than descriptions of an
actual physical space. Critic Andy Grundberg wrote in the *New
York Times* that, "The 'Equivalents' remain photography's most
radical demonstration of faith in the existence of a reality behind
and beyond that offered by the world of appearances. They are
intended to function evocatively, like music, and," as previously
cited, "they express a desire to leave behind the physical world,
a desire symbolized by the virtual absence of horizon and scale
clues within the frame. Emotion resides solely in form, they
assert, not in the specifics of time and place."[35] Kuster's imagery
of the sky also functions evocatively, eliciting reflection, but in
his case certain specifics are stamped onto each photograph,
including the estimated number of victims, further recalled by
the ambient tones.

●

In our digital era, photographs have become more quantum-
like, perceived as being more of what might have been and what
could be rather than reliable recordings of events and people.
This may be a necessary evolution given that, in a larger sense,
society's relationship to the real has evolved as well. As the
tech veteran, Mark Pesce, wrote in "The Last Days of Reality,"
a disturbing, 8,000-word essay published in 2017 that outlined
the era in which we now live, "...it's becoming increasingly
difficult to determine what in our interactions is simply human
and what is machine-generated. It is becoming difficult to know
what is real."[36] Or, as one user of such synthesizing software
commented, "If anything can be real, nothing is real."

But other forces are at work as well. The "reality-based community" is a phrase attributed by journalist Ron Suskind to an official in President George Bush's administration who used it to denigrate a critic of the government's policies as someone who bases their judgments on facts. In a 2004 article in the *New York Times Magazine*, Suskind wrote, "The aide said that guys like me were 'in what we call the reality-based community', which he defined as people who 'believe that solutions emerge from your judicious study of discernible reality'. [...] 'That's not the way the world really works anymore,' he continued. 'We're an empire now, and when we act, we create our own reality. And while you're studying that reality – judiciously, as you will – we'll act again, creating other new realities, which you can study too, and that's how things will sort out. We're history's actors...and you, all of you, will be left to just study what we do.'"[37]

The self-serving fantasy of the "empire" needs to be undercut and disputed, not transcribed. The staging of events for the press should be exposed and the manipulations behind the scenes made transparent; a second, more informative photograph can be used to deconstruct the staged one. Official platitudes need to be juxtaposed with imagery, properly contextualized, of the realities that they attempt to conceal. And the character of leaders needs to be interrogated in the portraits made of them rather than simply confirming their role.

It is a pivotal moment, as former German Chancellor Angela Merkel put it several years ago, commenting on the devastation in Syria. "When a free-trade agreement with the U.S.A. drives hundreds of thousands of people to the streets, but such horrible bombings as in Aleppo do not trigger any protest, then something is not right."[38] Or, as the critic Charles Simic more sardonically stated, "The world seems to be divided today between those horrified to see history repeat itself and those who eagerly await its horrors."[39]

Chapter Six

Synthetic Challenges

"A photograph of an unhappy algorithm."

This is a synthetic image, not a photograph, generated by DreamStudio in response to the text prompt (above) by the author, August 2023.

"Nonfiction photography is
a recording of the visible
in which the photographer
strives to represent actualities
(events, people, etc.) in a fair
and accurate manner with
appropriate context."

The Writing with Light campaign, 2024

Contrasting the emergence of artificial intelligence systems
with the invention of the horseless carriage, Microsoft's chief
economist, Michael Schwarz, suggested that we should wait
until we see "meaningful harm" from AI before we regulate it.
Comparing it to driver's licenses, which were introduced after
dozens of people were killed in automobile accidents, he stated:
"There has to be at least a little bit of harm so that we see what
is the real problem."[1]

That "little bit of harm" is now ubiquitous and self-evident.
As the *Washington Post* reported less than seven weeks after the
current Israel-Gaza conflict began, "A recent search for 'Gaza'
on Adobe Stock brought up more than 3,000 images labeled as
AI-generated out of some 13,000 total results. Several of the top
results appeared to be AI-generated images that were not labeled
as such, in apparent violation of the company's guidelines. They
included a series of images depicting young children, scared and
alone, carrying their belongings as they fled the smoking ruins of
an urban neighborhood."[2] This highly mediated conflict becomes,
partially as a result, one of the most confusing and opaque.

Similarly, the *Post* noted that "a search for 'Ukraine war' on
Adobe Stock turned up more than 15,000 fake images of the
conflict, including one of a small girl clutching a teddy bear
against a backdrop of military vehicles and rubble. Hundreds
of AI images depict people at Black Lives Matter protests that
never happened. Among the dozens of machine-made images
of the Maui wildfires, several look strikingly similar to ones
taken by photojournalists."

While several stock photography outlets are selling synthetic
imagery of this kind, it is noteworthy, as mentioned previously,
that Adobe is the company spearheading the Content
Authenticity Initiative which bills itself, it now seems somewhat
ironically, as "focus[ing] on systems to provide context and
history for digital media."[3]

This comes at a time when, according to a recent Pew Research Center study, half of Americans get their news at least sometimes from social media where editorial oversight is nearly non-existent, and a growing amount of synthetic imagery, often lurid and provocative, is to be found.[4] Simultaneously, recent surveys have found synthetic imagery to be regarded at times as more credible and even more trustworthy than photographs.[5] And for cash-strapped publications without robust ethical policies or experienced photo editors, these low-cost images used as illustrations become a way to help them survive financially.

In a similar vein, Google's recent announcement that its Search bar will allow artificial intelligence to fabricate some of the imagery that certain of its users request rather than finding photographs that already exist is portentous.[6] The eventual implications of this for the historical record can be serious, as photographs made over nearly 200 years are at risk of being supplanted as referents. As one reader of the *Washington Post* put it, "We are losing a whole category of evidence. We are losing one of the ways we have come to know the world. And we have nothing to put in its place."

We are, in the process, losing the sense of a shared reality. We are all encouraged to make our own, without much thought being given to the consequences. "This is the classic story of the last 20 years: unleash technology, invade everybody's privacy, wreak havoc, become trillion-dollar-valuation companies, and then say, 'Well, yeah, some bad stuff happened'... We're sort of repeating the same mistakes, but now it's supercharged because we're releasing this stuff on the back of mobile devices, social media, and a mess that already exists," asserts Hany Farid, a leading forensic scientist.[7]

The problem goes far beyond journalism. In 2022, high school students in upstate New York produced a short deepfake video of the school's principal uttering racist comments and asserting that he was going to bring a machine gun with him to school.

Although those responsible for the hoax had terrorized many members of the school community, the local police responded by saying that there was nothing they could do to punish the perpetrators.[8]

That same year, a woman leading a campaign against "revenge porn" also was herself depicted acting in a pornographic film, a form of abuse suffered by many women (nonconsensual deepfake pornographic videos almost exclusively target women) on websites dedicated to such malicious fakery. And as I write this, a newsletter from 404 Media has arrived announcing, "A Telegram user who advertises their services on Twitter will create an AI-generated pornographic image of anyone in the world for as little as $10 if users send them pictures of that person."[9] Previously, a 2024 Channel 4 News analysis in Britain of the five most visited deepfake websites, which received 100 million views in three months, found almost 4,000 famous individuals listed, including, as reported in the *Guardian,* "female actors, TV stars, musicians and YouTubers, who have not been named, whose faces were superimposed on to pornographic material using artificial intelligence."[10]

One of those victimized, Cathy Newman, who works for Channel 4 News as a presenter, responded: "It feels like a violation. It just feels really sinister that someone out there who's put this together, I can't see them, and they can see this kind of imaginary version of me, this fake version of me."[11]

Children are also being targeted, sometimes by their peers, in various locations. In 2023, more than twenty female students aged 11–17 from a little Spanish town appeared online nude; local boys aged 12 to 14 years had allegedly used photographs of the girls clothed to generate naked deepfakes. As a result, some of the girls were traumatized and unable to leave their homes. As the BBC reported: "We didn't know how many children had the images, if they had been uploaded to pornographic sites – we had all those fears," Dr. Miriam Al Adib, a gynecologist and one of the girls' mothers, stated in a video meant to reassure others affected. "When you are the victim of a crime, if you are robbed, for example, you file a complaint and you don't hide because the other person has caused you harm. But with crimes of a sexual nature the victim often feels shame and hides and feels responsible. So I wanted to give that message: it's not your fault."[12]

Most people do not have sufficient media literacy to understand how easily photographs or videos can be manipulated or simulated, and as a result, they lack the skepticism necessary to help undermine these attacks. And there is not enough psychological support for those who have been victimized. The lack of legal remedies and controls online will allow incidents like these to proliferate, including in much more vicious ways, targeting not only celebrities but one's fellow citizens as well.

The Web already contains many pornographic synthetic images and videos of children, some based on actual photographs of children who had previously been abused. While these have become easier to produce, the Internet was rife with such imagery even before the widespread emergence of image generators. "Facebook, for example, has a 'zero tolerance' policy for child sex material and reported more than 20 million such images in 2020," according to a 2023 column in *USA Today,* while "Google reported about 550,000 images the same year."[13] More recently, the National Center for Missing & Exploited Children, a US-based clearinghouse, "received 4,700 reports of images or videos of the sexual exploitation of children made by generative AI, a category it only started tracking in 2023."[14] Meanwhile, portals to the virtual world have increased dramatically. "In 2008 there was an average of one computer per household," it was reported in *The Hill* in 2023, while "today, families in the U.S. have an average of 20 Internet-capable devices."[15]

Over the last forty years, some steps have been taken to constrain and counteract digital media's ability to manipulate imagery: Google, for example, recently updated its cameras to produce more realistic skin tones for darker-skinned people. But these measures can be paltry and, at least in one case, may have made matters worse. France, Israel and Norway require advertisers to label advertising images in which the models' bodies have been modified to correct perceived "flaws" in their appearance, while other countries depend upon industry self-regulation in this regard. However, a major concern remains: the erosion of self-esteem in people who look at the media's thin and unrealistic images of women's bodies, a problem that can lead to an increase in eating disorders as people attempt to reshape their own bodies to look like the digitally manipulated models.

"It turns out women do not behave as the legislators have assumed," according to Marika Tiggemann, a professor at Flinders University who studies body image. "Disclaimer labels do not make women judge the image as any less realistic, and they do not make women compare any less with the model in the image. If anything, they tend to compare more."[16] The size or wording of the disclaimers seem to make no difference, and their inclusion can even worsen body dissatisfaction.

Why? Tiggemann points to several reasons, including the power of the image prevailing over the few words in the disclaimer (a similar concern with images labeled as having been generated by AI) and the lack of more specific information on how the initial photograph was changed. Her analysis is sobering: "Over time, I have come to the conclusion that, rather than being read as saying 'Don't compare yourself with these thin and unrealistic models,' disclaimer labels are actually read as saying something closer to 'It must be really important to be thin and attractive.' Given that disclaimer labels show that even the thin and very attractive bodies and faces of models need to be digitally corrected and enhanced, they are not going to make the owner of an 'average' body feel any better about their own body.

In this way, disclaimer labels may actually reinforce the narrow and rigid beauty ideals they are meant to undermine." A solution, she suggests, is to diversify the ways in which women's bodies are depicted in the media.

This can also be problematic. Rather than photographing more diverse models, artificial intelligence systems now can synthesize the images at a fraction of the cost, without having to pay either the models or photographers. At least one fashion company announced plans to do just that, defending their methodology as a way of increasing the number and diversity of the models they present when using real people would be too expensive. As a result, the illusion of diversity is sustained, but photographers and models, as well as their assistants and make-up artists, can be left unemployed.

Such tweaks also do not address the larger problems of racism, misogyny and cultural stereotyping embedded in artificial intelligence systems which have been trained on images that already reflect such biases. As the *Washington Post* recently demonstrated, the prompt "toys in Iraq" summons images of toy soldiers with guns. Plugging in "attractive people" returns pictures of the young and light-skinned. "Muslim people" appear as men with head coverings. As the *Post* characterized it, "Asian women are hypersexual. Africans are primitive. Europeans are worldly. Leaders are men. Prisoners are Black."[17] While considerable efforts have been made to address many of these biases in schools, museums, publications and elsewhere, a simple text prompt may see them resurface.

It is difficult to know which biases are being amplified in AI-generated content, according to Laura Ellis, the head of technology forecasting at the BBC, "because we simply don't know what datasets have been used to train these models."[18] More transparency would be helpful but, since tech companies are self-policing and governments have been reluctant to require such clarity, it's unlikely to happen.

In the meantime, a first step would be to teach media literacy as attentively as reading and writing. This would entail equipping young people with the skills to question all kinds of images, synthetic and photographic, for their abilities to stereotype and denigrate, as well as for their abilities to portray actual people and bear witness to events. This requires a balancing act and considerable guidance, which would be easier if the people who publish the imagery, particularly those running social media platforms, would take more responsibility for the material they distribute.

When Mark Zuckerberg shared a photo of his family on Instagram, he replaced his children's faces with happy face emojis. Zuckerberg, who owns Instagram, was illustrating two problems: the danger for those whose faces are shown on social media, and the tech giants' abnegation of responsibility to care for others. As Zoe Williams wrote in the *Guardian* at the beginning of 2024, "With each new threat, the prospect of a regulatory solution has looked ever more distant, as tech interests have run rings around legislators and nations have failed to cooperate around this essentially unborderable phenomenon. Besides, there was this human problem right at heart of it: how do you make truth, which is complicated and messy, more interesting than lies, which are bold and designed to be emotionally satisfying?"[19]

At an essential level, the digital revolution has helped to propel the reimagining of reality as a malleable construction to be deconstructed and overridden. Image-manipulation software began emerging in the late 1970s and early 1980s just as Cindy Sherman's series "Untitled Film Stills," a post-modern critique of cinematic constructs in which she styled herself as female characters from mid-century B movies, was first being exhibited. And it was the same time as Ronald Reagan, a former movie actor, was running for president of the United States, playing the role of a Hollywood cowboy in a ten-gallon hat riding a horse in front of news cameras.

The actual policies Reagan later put in place, like trickle-down economics, belied that populist performance and left many workers in economic distress. "It's morning again in America," a narrator pronounced four years later in one of the most influential campaign ads ever produced, extolling Reagan's success and blurring serious problems. "Today more men and women will go to work than ever before in our country's history," he continued. While delivered mellifluously, the increase in the workforce cited reflected the growth in the American population over four years while ignoring the rate of unemployment (at about 7.5 percent) that was higher than when Jimmy Carter, Reagan's predecessor, had left office.

Kickstarting a trend that has become considerably more exaggerated today, the illusion was what took precedence. "Set to the music of sentimental strings," as the New York Times described the ad, "images include a paperboy on his bicycle, a family taking a rolled rug into a house and campers raising an American flag. The subtext is that after 20 years of social tumult, assassinations, riots, scandal, an unpopular war and gas lines, Mr. Reagan returned the United States to the tranquility of the 1950s."[20] Now it is the news that is attacked as "fake" when it has been so often the political leaders' pronouncements that are devoid of substance.

In response, as picture editor of the New York Times Magazine when Reagan first took office, I had assigned the Brazilian Sebastião Salgado to photograph him for an article on the first hundred days of his presidency, wanting to have an observer on the scene who, living elsewhere, hadn't been influenced by the Marlboro Man-style campaign imagery that preceded his election.[21] But then, two years later, invited to the White House by Reagan's personal photographer, Michael Evans, and having not seen the president during my visit, I was informed that he had been practicing his hockey shot for the cameras. Reagan was, it seems, preparing for the visit of the victorious U.S. Olympic hockey team later that day. As a Time picture editor once described it to me, covering politics is like "photographing Hollywood movie sets."

Professional photographers continued to be complicit in such stagings, in a way that was similar to what John Szarkowski, former director of photography at New York's Museum of Modern Art, described them doing in the first century of their existence, "perform[ing] a role similar to that of the ancient scribe, who put in writing such messages and documents as the illiterate commoner and his often semiliterate ruler required."[22] The well-known photograph of President George W. Bush's 2003 appearance on the USS *Abraham Lincoln* in front of a "Mission Accomplished" sign, signaling the end of a conflict that was just beginning, is one of the most prominent examples of this continuing trend to substantiate pseudo-realities. It contributes, along with other such shortcuts, to the waning of the "reality-based community," as journalist Ron Suskind described it, so that in 2023 only 40 percent of 93,000 people worldwide who were surveyed said they trust most news most of the time, according to the Reuters Institute for the Study of Journalism, while "56 percent worry about identifying the difference between real and fake news on the internet."[23] Image generators, which allow such scenarios to be fashioned in seconds, can be made to produce this deceptive veneer at an unprecedented scale, making it even more urgent for visual journalists to find ways to unmask these pseudo-realities and restore the importance of the actual.

•

In 1982, coincidentally the year that the modified *National Geographic* cover of the pyramids of Giza was published, John Berger wrote in *Another Way of Telling*, "Photographs do not translate from appearances. They quote from them." And until recently, that was our understanding of how, at an essential level, photography functioned. But in the current age, we might want to think of the camera as more like a pen, and a photographer as an author akin to a writer.

After all, "photography" traces its etymology to writing or drawing with light, and this can lead to other ways of reconceiving its implementation. So that, for example, just as a writer of nonfiction can only use quotation marks when the words cited are the actual ones a person wrote or said, so too might journalistic or documentary photographers think of the frame as the quotation marks around the scene that appears in the viewfinder.

Rather than trying to determine a photograph's authenticity by counting the number of pixels that were modified by software, or searching through previous iterations of the same image for alterations, it would be simpler for the reader to be able to think of a photograph as a quotation from appearances, as Berger phrased it, with any major deviations from that role having to be indicated. Minor modifications – modestly changing the contrast, cropping the image, cleaning up digital "noise" (random pixels scattered through an image much like the static one might hear on the radio) – would be allowed. This would be equivalent to the latitude given to a writer to modify a quote by leaving out *ums* or *uhs*, deciding where to begin and end the quote, or to use an ellipsis to indicate words that have been removed from within a phrase. And in the same way that responsible writers of nonfiction are unable to insert words that a person did not say, a nonfiction photographer would not be allowed to add or subtract visual elements from a photograph, including people and objects. In all cases, for both the photographer and the writer, alterations would be forbidden if they changed the essential meanings of either the imagery or the words.

In 2023 the Writing with Light campaign was initiated by a group of photography professionals in collaboration with a few organizations, including World Press Photo, Magnum Photos, and the National Press Photographers Association. It was framed as "a movement to support nonfiction photography in which the integrity of the photographer, as the author of the image, is considered to be paramount in establishing the photograph's veracity."[24]

What is nonfiction photography? Unlike in a bookstore or
library where a demarcation between fiction and nonfiction is
evident (novels or poetry vs. history or science, for example),
in photography there has never been such a clear distinction
(documentary photography, as we have seen, may involve quite
a bit of staging and misdirection, and a fine art photograph
may itself be considered a documentary depiction of the
landscape or person who was in front of the lens). Working
with photojournalist Brian Palmer and the general counsel
to the National Press Photographers Association, Mickey H.
Osterreicher, we put forth a working definition of nonfiction
photography as "a recording of the visible in which the
photographer strives to represent actualities (events, people, etc.)
in a fair and accurate manner with appropriate context."

This follows, by nearly a century-and-a-half, the 1882 court case
that first established that photographs (in this case a portrait
of Oscar Wilde by Napoleon Sarony) could be copyrighted,
because it was decided that the images produced were created
by a human being and not simply the product of a machine.
The justices found the photographic portrait to be a "useful,
new, harmonious, characteristic, and graceful picture, and that
plaintiff made the same...entirely from his own original mental
conception, to which he gave visible form by posing the said
Oscar Wilde in front of the camera, selecting and arranging
the costume, draperies, and other various accessories in said
photograph, arranging the subject so as to present graceful
outlines, arranging and disposing the light and shade, suggesting
and evoking the desired expression, and from such disposition,
arrangement, or representation, made entirely by plaintiff,
he produced the picture in suit." This allowed the justices to
describe the photograph as an original work of art "for which
the Constitution intended that Congress should secure to him
the exclusive right to use, publish, and sell."[25]

Although not art, this notion that photojournalistic practice
is rooted in authorship is reflected in the Writing with Light

campaign. Journalistic or documentary photographers must be able to do more than illustrate preconceptions and please clients. If they choose a nonfiction practice, photographers are to be considered responsible for the interpretation of people and events expressed by the image and the way it is contextualized, rather than relying on the camera as the unchallenged arbiter of the real.

Many of the current efforts to safeguard the authenticity of the photograph rely on technology. For example, watermarking imagery that is generated by artificial intelligence can be helpful. The various AI companies could collaborate to decide on a single icon like a copyright symbol to indicate that an image is synthetic, rather than each creating their own. Still, such markings can frequently be removed or otherwise obscured, while people generating imagery from open-source systems may be able to circumvent these constraints.

The Content Authenticity Initiative, which cryptographically records any secondary modifications to the original, relies on technology to determine provenance and authenticity, but it is not foolproof. OpenAI, the company that owns the image generator DALL·E 3, as well as the chatbot, ChatGPT, has begun to use the Content Authenticity Initiative's system of metadata, called C2PA. But on its blog, OpenAI points to a major problem: "Metadata like C2PA is not a silver bullet to address issues of provenance. It can easily be removed either accidentally or intentionally. For example, most social media platforms today remove metadata from uploaded images, and actions like taking a screenshot can also remove it. Therefore, an image lacking this metadata may or may not have been generated with ChatGPT or our API."[26]

To authenticate an image, one would have to submit it to the Content Credentials Verify website, but without metadata this would not work. Despite these hurdles, OpenAI goes on to proclaim, "We believe that adopting these methods for

Oscar Wilde, photograph by Napoleon Sarony, 1882.

establishing provenance and encouraging users to recognize
these signals are key to increasing the trustworthiness of digital
information." This proclamation of good faith is common in the
industry, although the solutions proposed are generally far
from perfect.

Certainly, there are other ways to research the provenance of
an image, some used by forensic scientists, including reverse
image searching and comparing an image with others from the
same time and place. There are also websites and specialized

software that can help a viewer recognize fakery. But no system
can evaluate the masses of images that people confront every day
with any degree of certainty; one of the more frequent errors
is the misidentification of actual photographs as having been
produced by artificial intelligence. Baudelaire's admonition
that photography should strive to be no more than a recording
device to be utilized by "the secretary and clerk of whoever needs
an absolute factual exactitude in his profession" becomes an
increasingly uncertain proposition.

In the journalistic coverage of events, digital markers can
reassure editors as to the validity of the photographs they are
receiving, including where and when they were made and
whether they were subsequently modified. Along with other fact-
checking, this can help the editors decide whether to publish
the image. However, they may become over-reliant on those
photographers who can afford authenticating technologies and
exclude those without the necessary hardware or software, as
well as those who are in dangerous situations where they may
need to disconnect the system to camouflage their presence, and
non-professionals who just happen to be on the scene. And more
problematically, if photographers' central role as witness and
interpreter of events becomes dependent on the technical data
collected, their authorship can become secondary in determining
the photograph's value. For example, a photograph of an event
staged to look spontaneous could be labeled unmodified,
whereas a photograph of an actual event in which parts of the
sky are slightly darkened could be viewed as suspect.

A larger problem may emerge: readers might become so
skeptical of all photographs that they would feel compelled
to study the history of changes made to every image and
dismiss any that had been modified in even the most trivial,
and journalistically acceptable, way. They might not be literate
enough to differentiate essential fraud from slight changes
the photographer made to compensate for poor lighting or to
highlight a subject, or adjustments for odd colors from artificial

light sources, such as were commonly accepted in the film era. In the text world, a writer would not be expected to offer the reader the complete transcript of an interview after having quoted a sentence or two from it. It should still be possible to trust a serious photographer to work within specified limits, and editors to do their best to confirm the credibility of the imagery they publish.

Another strategy to bolster integrity and transparency would involve adding layers of context by using the digital possibilities of interactivity and multimedia, as well as the extraordinary resources of the Web, rather than concentrating on authenticating a photograph via technical means. An example of this is the Four Corners Project,[27] which I initially proposed in 2004 in Amsterdam during a keynote speech to the annual meeting of World Press Photo. Its purpose was to increase the context and credibility of the photograph online in ways that would be difficult or impossible to do on paper. It had occurred to me that, unlike print media, the online environment allows one to embed layers of information in the corners of a photograph. So I conceived of a template in which each of the photograph's four corners holds specific kinds of information that an interested reader can reveal by placing the cursor over it, allowing a photographer to complement the photograph with additional perspectives when desired.

In this configuration, the bottom left corner is for the Backstory, where the photographer puts text or audio explaining what was going on at the time the photograph was made. For example, one might imagine a description such as this, recorded by the photographer: "The politician had been shaking hands with all kinds of people for approximately 45 minutes when he stopped and picked up this baby I photographed. The baby's mother was not happy. She told me afterwards that they had been just walking by on the way to do grocery shopping at the supermarket." Related Imagery is situated in the upper left corner, allowing for photos, videos and drawings that explain more about the single photograph. For example, along with the photograph of the drowned two-year-old child Alan Kurdi, one might choose to show him with his family on a holiday, or with his brother, who also drowned, when they were playing with a stuffed animal. The additional images would give readers a sense of the normalcy and joy in his life, and compare it to their own, rather than defining him only by his status as a refugee or by his death.

Links, located in the upper right corner, points to other websites that explain more about what is going on, adding to the information that a photographer appends to the photo. There, the reader could put links to maps, histories of the region or biographical information about a person, news articles, or to the photographer's home page containing a larger body of work on the same subject and on others. Authorship, in the bottom right corner of the photograph, is where the photographer can write a caption for the photograph, place the credit and copyright information (or use Creative Commons), include a short bio indicating experience in the field that may be

The template for the Four Corners Project, which allows a reader to
retrieve different kinds of information from each corner of the photograph.

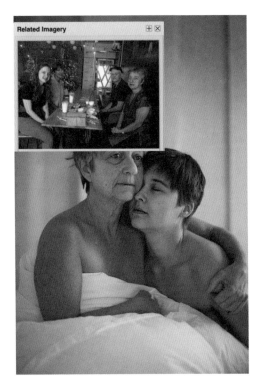

The Four Corners Project is used here to show the photographer
Nora Savosnick with her mother when she was ill, and then
to reveal "Related Imagery" of their family together.

relevant, and also contact information for a viewer who wants
to obtain reproduction rights or buy a print. This bolsters the
photographer's status as an author and potentially leads to
further publication and even remuneration.

Here the photographer can also provide a personal code of
ethics in two or three informative sentences. For example,
a photojournalist might write: "While all photography is
interpretive, as a photojournalist my photographs are meant
to respect the visible facts of the situations I depict. I do not
add or subtract elements to or from my photographs." Or a fine
art photographer: "I may alter my images in pursuit of my own

artistic vision." A photographer working both as an artist and
a journalist might say: "This is an artistic image, allowing me
to take liberties in altering the photograph. I do not alter my
journalistic imagery." And there may be special cases, such as:
"While on assignment for UNICEF, I abide by UNICEF's code
of ethics. I do not show the faces of children who are HIV-
positive or who have been child soldiers." Photographers with
various specialties can do the same: "As a fashion photographer,
I do not photograph underweight models whose Body Mass
Index is lower than that established as healthy by authorities."
There is also space to compose one's own code of ethics.

When I proposed this template to the World Press Photo annual
gathering, the assembled photographers, editors, and agents
responded with enthusiastic applause. Yet no one did anything
to move the idea forward. Some fifteen years later, I received
a small grant to hire a young website developer, Corey Tegeler,
to build the software, while Perri Hofmann managed the
project and contributed to its design, and various ex-students
and others translated the instructions into several languages.
It has been online and free to use at fourcornersproject.org for
several years, yet despite many lectures throughout the world
advocating its use and my attempts to interest tech organizations
and publications, with the notable exception of a recent project
initiated by the Starling Lab for Data Integrity in conjunction
with the Bay City News Foundation to document homelessness
in the San Francisco area, there have been very few adoptees
and no effort to integrate it more broadly into other popular
templates that already exist.

Now, even as companies such as Google and Adobe seek to
inform the viewer of the origins of a photograph, and with
reverse image searches available such as Tin Eye, there
has been little interest in giving photographers a way to
contextualize their own imagery, the product of a fractional
second. The possible insights from the photograph's authors,
subjects, and eyewitnesses are not seen as valuable. Even as

masses of manipulated and decontextualized images are available online, and photographs are now simulated by artificial intelligence, photographers are rarely given a greater role in adding to and authenticating what they witnessed. Instead, it is technology that is called upon to fix a problem that has been largely created by other technologies that we have invented.

The challenges for artists using synthetic imagery are quite different, of course, given that the credibility of witnessing is not as relevant to their work. Some of the challenges are, instead, defensive: preventing artificial intelligence systems from scraping artists' imagery online to collect the data for training, including with legal threats and with software. Nightshade, for example, is a software in development that can intentionally "poison" an artist's images before uploading them by imperceptibly modifying pixels to skew the AI systems that may scrape their work. Another, Glaze, "masks" an artist's personal style so that the artificial intelligence cannot learn to imitate it.

Already, some are feeling sidelined – text prompts that ask for images *in the style of* a particular artist or designer can lead to a loss of income. While some companies have taken steps to combat this, and certain artists and photographers or their representatives are suing for compensation, there's a lack of clarity in both legal and ethical terms. Most prominently, in early 2023 Getty Images filed a lawsuit yet to be resolved alleging that Stability AI had copied without permission more than 12 million of its photographs, along with captions and metadata, as part of an attempt to create a competing business. The lawsuit asks for damages of up to $150,000 for each work that had been utilized, an amount that could add up to $1.8 trillion. Later that year Getty announced its own synthetic imaging service, Generative AI by Getty Images, this time with the stated intention of indemnifying contributors for the use of their photographs as training data.

Making photorealistic synthetic imagery "in the style" of particular photographers is a contentious issue, just as it is for writers, painters, musicians, and others. While few creators would deny that they have been influenced by others, image generation in response to a text prompt is different, largely outside of the control of the one writing the prompts, with a tendency, at least at this point, to imitate styles rather than transform them according to a second artist's vision. Could synthesizing photorealistic imagery in the style of non-photographers – writers, physicists, musicians, philosophers – be considered more experimental and spiritually resonant, given that no extant photographs exist to scrape and remake? A promise of the digital environment is that the source code of a digitized painting, let's say, can be output as music, or vice versa. Might there be interesting synchronicities to discover, or duets among different disciplines that might never have been attempted? The strategies here, while still needing to be evaluated as such experiments continue, can resemble an attempt at understanding and inspiration rather than appropriation.

The far greater goal than simulating previous media would be to use artificial intelligence to do what these media cannot do, visualizing worlds imagined and previously unseen by using algorithms to produce environments that resonate with the particular artist's vision. And as the paradigm shifts and generative AI's capabilities become clearer, previous media can be re-thought and used in more expansive ways, just as photography liberated painters to make imagery that was less representational, more emotional and abstract.

At this point some may be inclined to be skeptical of media in general, but wholesale denials can also lead to living in a bubble of one's own making. It is as if each person can now have a custom-made lens that configures the world as he or she pleases, with algorithms trained to select and synthesize only what a person wants to see. The situation begins to resemble the vision of cyborg pioneer Steve Mann, who suggested that the computer could be trained to remove content from a person's visual environment via a head-mounted display, so that a poster of a semi-nude woman advertising a Caribbean vacation, for example, might be automatically erased from the scene for those who find such sexualized imagery objectionable. (This is not unlike AI systems that blur image results that the algorithms find to be objectionable, such as for nudity.)

While it's an intriguing idea, given the contemporary image overload, the strategy of what is called "diminished reality" could be applied in other, more objectionable ways: perhaps to unhoused people sitting on the sidewalk, for example, going so far as to replace them with an image of something less challenging. The computer might then be made to produce what could be thought of as a kind of visual dystopia, selectively lightening or darkening skin colors, making the world conform to one's prejudices not only on a computer screen in the home or office, but on the street via one's eyeglasses as well.

This kind of fictional overlay could become a palatable alternative for those to whom the screen already has primacy. In a much milder way, this already happens with televised events where advertising signage in a stadium can be substituted for far-away viewers; even hospitals use simulated scenes of the outdoors intended to speed up patient recovery in windowless rooms.

The masses of synthetic and manipulated imagery being uploaded online have already, in their abundance, made much of our purview a "diminished reality" in which it is difficult to tell what has been reconfigured or erased. Henry Luce's 1936 prospectus for what would become *Life*, exploiting photography's new portability, today seems both naive and even quixotic: "To see life; to see the world; to eyewitness great events... To see and to show is the mission now, for the first time, undertaken by a new kind of publication."[28]

An alternative proposal for today might be: can we, equipped with the most sophisticated technology, find ways to share our insights and observations while seeking out new ones rather than limiting our purview to an increasingly artificial world?

"A[n] iconic photograph that is so horrible it would cause wars to stop," inspired by the work of the photographer Robert Capa.

Chapter Seven

Shifting Paradigms

"If the doors of perception were cleansed every thing would appear to man as it is, Infinite. For man has closed himself up, till he sees all things thro' narrow chinks of his cavern."

William Blake, *The Marriage of Heaven and Hell*, 1790

In a world replete with virtual reality, augmented reality, mixed reality, and diminished reality, as well as the massive potential of artificial intelligence to synthesize new realities, what we lack is a shared reality. Sharing was, of course, a crucial function of the photograph.

The malleability of the image, the shrinking of print media that could previously help societies to focus, the omnipresence of cameras and the new democracy of publishing that gives nearly anyone a platform, and now, the emergence of AI-generated imagery that can make anything appear to have happened, have all contributed to this fragmentation of a common reality. Consumer capitalism's capacity to cull an individual from the flock is responsible too. Its ability to seduce people into believing that their own needs and desires count the most, while simultaneously awarding them a stake in an online world, encourages a quick departure from the physical one, its complexities rendered too daunting to confront.

So it is no surprise that a photography engaged with that which exists independent of our desires is being abandoned, its imagery modified to conform to the way we think the world should be or overwritten with synthetic visions of what does not exist. Rather than referents, the photographs serve as "desirents," the camera and its software, or the image generators, functioning as post-photographic genies that can grant an abundance of wishes to re-make the world in our own image.

Altering or synthesizing photographs provides a sense of control when our universe seems chaotic. When we can enhance or simulate the photograph, the problematic world may seem less real and threatening, its realities dissipated. And, during the nearly seven hours a day people are said to spend online, that world can seem to go away.

Earlier this century, when smartphone cameras introduced lenses that looked backwards at the photographer instead of

forward to the larger world, a culture emerged in which the
photographer became both author and, explicitly, the subject,
closing the loop. The camera became more of a retouchable
mirror with which to join an online world, the other side of the
looking glass. In the late 1970s, the cultural critic Christopher
Lasch wrote of the beleaguered narcissists among us, buffeted
by a competitive, consumerist society, who have become unable
to "distinguish between themselves and the world beyond and
so have come to 'see the world as a mirror, more particularly as
a projection of one's own fears and desires.'"[1] The online world
becomes, for many, their corroboration and escape.

The 2006 cover image for *Time* featured "You" as the Person
of the Year, depicting a computer screen with Mylar on it,
so that readers could see themselves in the reflection. Here
the mirror was meant as celebratory. "You. You control the
Information Age. Welcome to your world," was the cover line,
somehow turning "users" into masters of their own destiny,
even though they were essentially feeding a machine so that
others could become unimaginably rich.

"The idea was that in the age of emerging social media, content
creators were changing the world," as Richard Stengel, *Time's*
managing editor, would later describe it. "Instead of the few
creating for the many, the many now create for one another."[2]

However, few people today would agree that individuals
"control the Information Age." Instead, we become addicted
to the screens we frequent, helping to train the sophisticated
algorithms by our choices while, in effect, being trained by them.
We are directed to read and look at what is often fabricated
and incendiary, as well as harmful to our health, to buy what
we don't need, and to anxiously wait for a small signal – a text,
an email, a beep, a "like" – that someone or something cares
about us. Stengel acknowledged that: "If I got anything wrong,
it was in not anticipating the downside of this new information
calculus, the rise of hate speech and disinformation, and how

a democratized system could be used against the very idea of democracy."[3] These are hardly small omissions.

Traditionally, documentary photographers have tried to explore what is happening in the world outside of themselves, rather than using the camera primarily as a mirror. Some have chosen a life's work reporting on injustices that they hoped to help correct by making them vivid and palpable, difficult to ignore. But now that catastrophic imagery is shown repeatedly, much of it lacking context and some of it concocted, with little sense of what can be done to alleviate the pain, the situations that photographs are meant to represent start to blur and seem more distanced.

Why should a photographer continue as a witness, especially when journalists are increasingly targeted and killed? As a colleague recently suggested, partly tongue in cheek, why not just synthesize imagery of a war zone rather than having to assign photographers and put them in harm's way? It is cheaper and, if one is focused on advancing a particular point of view, easier to control. And one can argue that synthesizing imagery from the points of view of eyewitnesses can be an important way to engage the perspectives of those who were directly involved. In a post-truth era, the ability of a photographer to help define a situation as an independent arbiter will hardly be taken for granted.

Serious photographers today will have to reconsider their mission in light of the changing culture. They need to commit to a transparency that clarifies their strategies for the reader and provides more context to anchor and augment the photograph. Staged events constructed to appear spontaneous would become a thing of the past; the old slogan of "f8 and be there" – just set the camera's aperture and photograph – would need to be only the starting point. And as the older paradigms shift, new opportunities emerge.

The text prompt generating the image that begins this chapter seemed an appropriate way to invoke and honor Robert Capa's

legacy. A dedicated humanist and anti-fascist who covered
five wars from the 1930s to 1954, making highly celebrated
photographs of the Spanish Civil War and the D-Day invasion
during World War II, Capa was killed in Indochina after stepping
on a landmine while photographing the conflict. He was forty
years old. "The war photographer's most fervent wish is for
unemployment," he once said. "It is not always easy to stand
aside and be unable to do anything except record the suffering
around one."[4]

Seventy years later, the image that resulted from my text prompt
drawing on Capa's work, "An iconic photograph that is so
horrible it would cause wars to stop," circumvents any emphasis
on spectacle, making the viewer not a voyeur but a participant
called upon to resolve its ambiguity and, crucially, one of those
now charged with ending any war that could be so unspeakably
dreadful. We are asked to visualize a horror that can deform a
camera and terrorize a child without requiring the photographer
to provide it for us.

This image, although synthetic, responds to an important
conundrum that John Berger identified in his 1972 essay,
"Photographs of Agony," focusing on the work of Don McCullin,
who like Capa had covered many wars, including, in McCullin's
case, the one in Vietnam. "McCullin's most typical photographs
record sudden moments of agony – a terror, a wounding, a death,
a cry of grief," Berger wrote. "These moments are in reality
utterly discontinuous with normal time." But the viewer, Berger
argued, does not realize this, and can view his response to this
sense of discontinuity as a failure. It becomes a sign of "his own
personal moral inadequacy" that "may now shock him as much
as the crimes being committed in the war."[5]

That shock in the photograph creates spectacle without context;
it does not situate the event in the system, political or economic,
responsible for it. And rather than provoking the viewer to
investigate the causes of the violence depicted and assign the

blame to those responsible, it leads the reader to feel guilty and ultimately powerless, able to do little more than contribute to charity. This is why, Berger asserts, such photographs "can be published with impunity."

In the synthetic image that my prompt returned there is not the same moment of discontinuity – instead, an ongoing concern elicited by a moment of agony that has not been delineated or described. Rather than succumbing to the feeling of helplessness, the reader is provoked to respond by asking what is happening, why don't I know about it, and how can I help, while implicitly encouraged to think about the systems that make it so difficult to ameliorate the horrors that confront us. What we are being shown here is not a photograph depicting an event to be seen as the past, but something that continues into the future, as do the possibilities for engagement with it.

The image is consonant with Nelba Márquez-Greene's suggestion that I previously cited, when she reflected on the tragic loss of her daughter, Ana Grace, in a school shooting nearly ten years previously. Responding to requests for autopsy photos, she wrote, "What did they think a photo could do that the truth of the tragedy had not already conveyed?" Her advice: "Lower your gaze and do the work without asking for any more blood from me."

While a photograph could never be taken at face value, now each image may need to be considered for what it obscures and leaves out. An increasing number of photographers have adopted a largely conceptual approach to documentary photography, insisting that their images be interrogated and exposed to find the systems underlying them. Works by Laia Abril on rape and abortion, Mari Batashevski on intertwined state and corporate power, Debi Cornwall on torture at Guantanamo, Diana Matar on police shootings, and Trevor Paglen on surveillance as well as on the training data and biases of computer vision, all ask the viewer to see what is not being shown. Their approaches represent a shift in perspective that acknowledges that the traditional bond between the camera and the realities that surround us is fraught, and the image that results can be constructed to camouflage more than reveal. The assumptions implicit in the act of photography become part of the critique. Returning to Capa, it is his much-cited mantra, "if your pictures aren't good enough, you aren't close enough," that needs rewriting, stressing the distance that may be necessary to elide the drama of the initial confrontation in order to broaden and rephrase the purpose of the photographic act.

Rather than simulating the photographic, a responsible use of artificial intelligence could help to explore the questions provoked by these images, filling in the lacunae with research into histories and impacts that may not immediately seem to be in concert with a viewer's interests. The frame then becomes more permeable and, given the digital mosaic, the image itself can be made interactive, to serve as a kind of menu leading to pathways of inquiry that AI supplies to amplify and interrogate the photographer's work.

Perhaps we can think of this as a kind of meta-photography, the image serving as a portal. It is neither a window nor a mirror, as John Szarkowski conceptualized the difference between documentary and art photography in his 1978 landmark exhibition,[6] but a door that can be opened to investigate what lies behind it. It is similar, although in a more pragmatic and less grandiose sense, to what William Blake suggested in 1790, half a century before photography was invented: "If the doors of perception were cleansed every thing would appear to man as it is, Infinite. For man has closed himself up, till he sees all things thro' narrow chinks of his cavern."[7]

What then can synthetic imagery do? We tend to overlook AI's ability to surprise with new ideas, some of them serendipitous. Rather than thinking of AI as a tool akin to software designed to accomplish specific tasks, we can invite it to collaborate on outlining possibility, circumventing assumptions while helping redefine aspects of our worldview. Just as photography was able to function dialectically, challenging the expectations of the photographer and the viewer with the evidence of the lens, synthetic imagery can reimagine possibilities. It can make viewers aware of their own limited perspectives and prejudices – even though it can also suggest outcomes that are banal and destructive. It's necessary, as with any medium, to be circumspect.

Freed from the limitations of visual realism, AI can draw on its vast banks of accumulated data to circumvent truisms, opening up a wide, hybridized range of possibilities based on diverse sources and conceptual approaches, including some that have fallen out of favor. The resulting imagery may elicit, for example, a quantum worldview over a Newtonian one, exploring parallel universes rather than a more conventional representation of cause and effect. Perhaps it will help us to better understand the paradox of our times, when logic and pragmatism are abandoned, facts are viewed as irrelevant, and truths are personal and irreconcilable. Can artificial intelligence help us to analyze and reconfigure the world in a way that might lead to greater coherence?

Since it does not require an actual subject, AI can explore not only what is, but what might be. It can riff on ideas, thoughts and dreams, the future and distant past, the whimsical and the far away. And since it is capable of visualizing data from other sources, its depictions may at times seem weighty enough to be taken seriously, even urgent. Using scientific data to generate imagery that describes the eventual ravages of climate change may prove to be essential for human survival, leading to action to diminish or even avoid the worst outcomes. So too, images that those suffering from trauma might generate to share what happened to them could become useful not only for them but for police and psychologists, for lawyers and judges, as well as for the general public. In scientific research, generating images of possible planets or medicines, prehistoric creatures or future ones, may lead to essential discoveries, some of them lifesaving.

"Compliant Detainee Media Room, Camp 5." Photograph by Debi Cornwall, 2014.

"Smoke Break, Camp America." Photograph by Debi Cornwall, 2014.

Both images from *Welcome to Camp America: Inside Guantánamo Bay* (Radius Books, 2017).

AI might also serve as a curatorial agent exploring the billions
of images that are produced daily and presenting those
that deserve more attention. It can be asked to show only
photographs or videos that have been made by insiders, rather
than tourists who have stayed somewhere for a short time, or vice
versa. It can be asked to present only those images made during
weekdays, or only on holidays. Or it can comb social media
for unique, idiosyncratic perspectives that never accumulated
enough "likes" to be appreciated by a wider audience, as well
as for photographs made by reputable photographers with long
track records working for respected publications that merit
broader attention. And it can search for those images that have
been watermarked or annotated to indicate how they were made
and whether they were modified and, although hardly foolproof,
alleviate some of the confusion around them.

AI also presents uniquely controversial challenges, such as the
ability to speak with dead relatives or friends, as cited previously,
via videos trained by artificial intelligence so that conversations
can continue, even advice dispensed, post-mortem. After having
been filmed by twenty synchronized cameras as she was asked
questions using StoryFile, a system created by her son, Marina
Smith MBE, an eighty-seven-year-old Holocaust educator in
England was cremated, and then those attending the funeral
were able to ask her questions. She answered them "with new
details and honesty," according to her son, Dr. Stephen Smith,
talking about things that she had previously kept private.
"Relatives were staggered by my mum's new honesty at her
funeral. She had previously been too embarrassed to reveal her
true childhood," said Smith, who is StoryFile's CEO. "A question
about it at the funeral suddenly had her revealing her childhood
in India that we knew nothing about."[8]

The ethical questions around this process are concerning, as
previously discussed, including how it affects the survivors and
respects the rights of the deceased. Also, some of the responses
may be problematic given AI's tendency at times to hallucinate,

Singleton/SBWASS-R1 and Three Unidentified Spacecraft (Space Based Wide Area Surveillance System; USA 32), 2012, from Trevor Paglen's "The Other Night Sky," an ongoing project to track and photograph the world of secret satellites. © Trevor Paglen. Courtesy the Artist, Altman Siegel, San Francisco and Pace Gallery.

making up answers that are inappropriate. Acknowledging some of these issues, HereAfter AI's model, rather than utilizing whatever digital footprint that is left behind to reanimate the deceased, "relies solely on consent from users," according to *EuroNews*, "who must opt-in to be interviewed and can choose who they share their 'life story avatar' with."[9]

The AI reanimation of the voices of six students killed by gun violence was recently used to try and convince members of the U.S. Congress to take action on gun control. It included the voice of ten-year-old Uzi Garcia, who was killed at school on May 22,

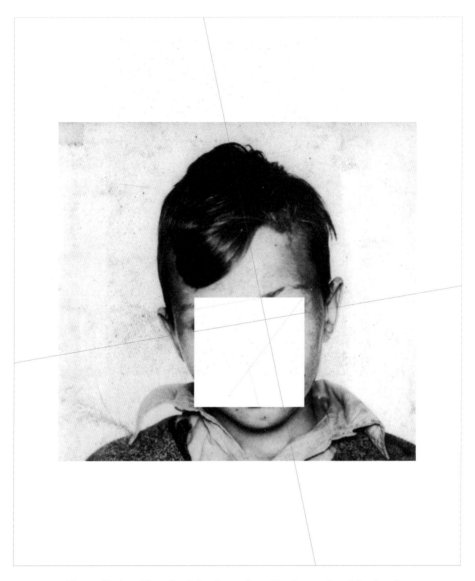

Trevor Paglen, They Took the Faces from the Accused and the Dead...
(#00520_1_F), 2019. Pigment print, 127.00 × 106.68 cm (50 × 42 in). © Trevor
Paglen. Courtesy the Artist, Altman Siegel, San Francisco and Pace Gallery

Trevor Paglen, Installation view "Uncanny Valley: Being Human in the Age of AI" at de Young Fine Arts Museum of San Francisco, 2020. Photo Randy Dodson. Image courtesy the Fine Arts Museums of San Francisco.

2022. As reported by CNN, Uzi's AI-generated voice says: "I love video games, telling jokes and making my friends laugh and jumping on the trampoline with my family. I'm a fourth grader at Robb Elementary School in Uvalde, Texas. Or at least I was when a man with an AR-15 came into my school and killed 18 of my classmates, two teachers, and me. That was almost two years ago. Nothing has changed. Even more shootings have happened."[10] Responding to criticism, Uzi's father, Brett Cross, told the news outlet, "If you think it's uncomfortable hearing my son's voice after he's passed, imagine what it's like to be us – to live with this every day."

Manuel Oliver, another father of a child killed at school, explained why he and his wife, Patricia, decided to recreate the voice of their son Joaquin, who died in Parkland, Florida, in 2018: "My wife and I have been trying to use our voices for the last six years. Nonstop. We have tried almost every single way to approach gun violence in a way that people will pay attention. We haven't been very successful," he said. "So we decided, you know what? Let's bring the voices of our loved ones. Let's bring the voice of Joaquin."

The group of parents also created a website, The Shotline, where their children's AI-generated voices can be heard "so they can call our representatives in hopes of changing our country's gun laws."[11] Reportedly, over 100,000 calls have been made.

Crossing another boundary, this time between internal thought processes and the outside world, as touched upon earlier, it's now possible to produce images of what people are visualizing by measuring the activity of their brains. This work has used Functional Magnetic Resonance Imaging (fMRI) with some 75 percent accuracy, comparing the image a person is looking at with the visual output from their brain. More recently Meta has announced an Image Decoder that uses a non-invasive neuroimaging technique, magnetoencephalography, and is able to reconstruct visual imagery from brain activity in real time using artificial intelligence.[12]

While advances like these can be useful for those who cannot speak because of a medical condition such as a stroke, and can potentially help scientists to visualize the ways in which animals perceive the world, the methodology raises issues of privacy. In a recent book, *The Battle for Your Brain: Defending the Right to Think Freely in the Age of Neurotechnology*, Duke University professor Nita Farahany finds it imperative that lawmakers act quickly to protect the human mind from unwanted intrusions to safeguard our personal liberty. As she argues on her website, "Our brain is our last bastion of freedom, our last place for privacy."[13]

Another possibility some have previously explored may be using AI systems to generate new imagery from our DNA. Digital media emerged at the same time as the discovery of DNA, which helped us see ourselves as code-based, and this conflation of code could encourage projects that resonate in both art and science, ways of understanding our deeper selves in new ways. Of course, there are ethical challenges, some of which are explored in Paul Virilio's 2000 *The Information Bomb*,[14] where he raises the possibility that people might be targeted according to segments of their DNA, a pointed and terrifying manifestation of eugenics.

Undoubtedly, artificial intelligence will be useful in multiple ways, leading to significant advances in nearly every sector of society, helping to create new medicines while also diagnosing diseases earlier, aiding in the exploration of ancient histories as well as in predicting future developments. In visual media, the ways in which AI can help to amplify our vision rather than undermine it will continue to emerge. And photographers, prodded by these new possibilities, can implement strategies that continue to acknowledge photography's role as a critical witness, doing so while providing more transparency and context as well as engaging more deeply with a greater diversity of perspectives, including those from the insiders who may understand their situation the best.

More self-consciously and with greater purpose, photography then can be a way to celebrate, criticize, and explore, rather than modify and enhance, all that is authentic within and around us. Chastened by challenges to its relevance, it can be rethought in more responsible and sober ways. We can then use artificial intelligence to investigate what is outside of photography's ken, and also to make sense of the trillions of images that have been made while, within constraints, helping to contextualize what they depict.

A critical, even at times skeptical approach to what a photograph represents has always been advisable. Now, in the age of image, it has become obligatory, just as targeted campaigns of disinformation have destabilized what we once thought of as the age of information. The viewer is left with the burden of having to collaborate in this process of deciphering which images can be trusted, and to what extent. As the Hungarian artist László Moholy-Nagy stated last century, "The illiterate of the future will be the person ignorant of the use of the camera as well as the pen." To that, we will have to add the image generators that produce much of today's still and moving imagery, facilitated by AI.

I am left asking if the synthetic image shown at the beginning of this chapter, a response by artificial intelligence to a text prompt that I provided invoking Robert Capa's celebrated work as a war photographer who wanted to end war, has co-opted his legacy or managed to extend it. My sense now is that, when done with transparency and respect, there is more that can still be said.

All the images in this portfolio are synthetic, not photographs, generated with artificial intelligence in response to a text prompt by the author.

"A photograph of a female peace photographer."

This is a synthetic image, not a photograph, generated by DreamStudio
in response to the text prompt (above) by the author, August 2023.

"A respectful photograph."

This is a synthetic image, not a photograph, generated by DreamStudio
in response to the text prompt (above) by the author, September 2023.

"A photograph of a dream in which two children
are playing with a ball on top of a lake."

This is a synthetic image, not a photograph, generated by DALL·E
in response to the text prompt (above) by the author, October 2022.

"A photograph of David vanquishing Goliath."

This is a synthetic image, not a photograph, generated by DreamStudio
in response to the text prompt (above) by the author, August 2023.

"A photograph of Adam and Eve and the apple of knowledge."

This is a synthetic image, not a photograph, generated by DreamStudio
in response to the text prompt (above) by the author, August 2023.

"A photograph of the Salem witches
on trial in 1692."

This is a synthetic image, not a photograph, generated by DreamStudio
in response to the text prompt (above) by the author, August 2023.

"Romantic Martians in love,"
inspired by the work of Virginia Woolf.

"The first photograph ever made."

This is a synthetic image, not a photograph, generated by DreamStudio
in response to the text prompt (above) by the author, August 2023.

"A photograph of an unhappy bot."

This is a synthetic image, not a photograph, generated by DreamStudio
in response to the text prompt (above) by the author, August 2023.

"A hopeful photograph made in 2050."

This is a synthetic image, not a photograph, generated by DreamStudio
in response to the text prompt (above) by the author, August 2023.

"A Pictorialist photograph of what one
first sees after one's own death."

This is a synthetic image, not a photograph, generated by DALL·E
in response to the text prompt (above) by the author, March 2023.

"A [P]ictorialist photograph
of a world without images."

This is a synthetic image, not a photograph, generated by DALL·E
in response to the text prompt (above) by the author, March 2023.

PREFACE

1   Cited in Jonathan Freedland, "The future of AI is chilling," the *Guardian,* May 26, 2023; original on X, Sia Kordestani, March 29, 2023.

2   Fred Ritchin, "Photography's New Bag of Tricks," the *New York Times Magazine,* November 4, 1984.

3   Carol Squiers, "Decisive Moments," *American Photo,* September/October 1997.

4   Frederick Kaufman, "Graciela Iturbide," *Aperture,* Winter 1995.

5   Ian Bogost, "Your Phone Wasn't Built for the Apocalypse," *The Atlantic,* September 11, 2020.

6   Jean-Pierre Isbouts, "Why Adam and Eve were cast out of Eden," *National Geographic,* January 31, 2019.

7   Jorge Luis Borges, "The Aleph," in *The Aleph and Other Stories* (London: Penguin Classics, 2004).

8   Roland Barthes, *Camera Lucida: Reflections on Photography* (New York: Hill and Wang, 1980).

CHAPTER ONE

1   Italo Calvino, "The Adventures of a Photographer," published in *The Short Story and Photography, 1880's-1980's: A Critical Anthology,* edited by Jane M. Rabb (Albuquerque: University of New Mexico Press, 1998). In this collection it was called "The Adventures of a Photographer," but the story is more commonly titled with the singular "Adventure."

2   "The internet is vicious and toxic, but I'd never go back to the 90s': Taylor Lorenz talks to Monica Lewinsky," the *Guardian,* October 5, 2023.

3   "Scarlett Johansson on fake AI-generated sex videos: 'Nothing can stop someone from cutting and pasting my image,'" the *Washington Post,* December 31, 2018.

4   Charles Baudelaire, "On Photography," from The Salon of 1859, *Charles Baudelaire:*

The Mirror of Art (Jonathan Mayne, editor; London: Phaidon Press Limited, 1955).

5   Shimrit Ben-Yair, "Magic Editor in Google Photos: New AI editing features for reimagining your photos," Google blog, May 10, 2023.

6   Jaron Schneider, "Google Photos Will Let You Completely Change Your Pictures with AI," *PetaPixel,* May 10, 2023.

7   Stephen Shankland, "How Close Is That Photo to the Truth? What to Know in the Age of AI," CNET, November 18, 2023.

8   Susan Sontag, *On Photography* (New York: Farrar, Straus and Giroux, 1977).

9   Stephen Mayes, "The Next Revolution in Photography is Coming," *Time,* August 25, 2015.

10 Shankland, *ibid.*

11 Vann Vicente, "What is Computational Photography?" How-To Geek, January 19, 2021.

12 Geoffrey A. Fowler, "Your smartphone photos are totally fake – and you love it," the *Washington Post,* November 14, 2018.

13 Michael Ignatieff, "The Reluctant Imperialist," the *New York Times,* August 6, 2000.

14 Jacques Rancière, *The Emancipated Spectator* (New York: Verso Books, 2008).

15 Jim Casper, "Another America – AI-Generated Photos from the 1940s and 50s," *LensCulture,* 2023.

16 *The Today Show* Adobe Photoshop Debut, https://www.youtube.com/watch?v=OHbM4QJYVYM

17 Dwight Silverman, "From darkrooms to Photoshop to Pixel 8's AI, trust has always been a photography issue," *Houston Chronicle,* December 18, 2023.

18 *The Today Show* Adobe Photoshop Debut, *ibid.*

19 August Sander, "Seeing, Observing and Thinking," Document REWE library,

Die Photographische Stiftung/ SK Stiftung Kultur – August Sander Archive, Köln. English translation by Shaun Whiteside, Sander Archive, November 1927.

20 Geoffrey Fowler, "Flawless or Fake? Google's AI now fixes smiles," the *Washington Post,* October 11, 2023.

21 Deepti Hajela, "Delete a background? Easy. Smooth out a face? Seamless. Digital photo manipulation is now mainstream," AP News, March 13, 2024.

CHAPTER TWO

1   Charles Baudelaire, "On Photography," from The Salon of 1859, *Charles Baudelaire: The Mirror of Art* (Jonathan Mayne, editor; London: Phaidon Press Limited, 1955).

2   William Carlos Williams, from "Asphodel, That Greeny Flower," *Journey to Love* (New York: Random House, 1955).

3   https://generated.photos

4   "After Walker Evans: 2," metmuseum.org.

5   Andy Grundberg, "Photography View: Stieglitz Felt the Pull of Two Cultures," the *New York Times,* February 13, 1983.

6   Susan Sontag, *On Photography* (New York: Farrar, Straus and Giroux, 1977).

7   Kevin Kelly, "Gossip is Philosophy," *Wired,* May 1, 1995.

8   Fred Ritchin, "Photography's New Bag of Tricks," the *New York Times Magazine,* November 4, 1984.

CHAPTER THREE

1   Melissa Heikkilä, "Nobody knows how AI works," *MIT Technology Review,* March 5, 2024.

2   Prabhakar Raghavan, "Gemini image generation got it wrong. We'll do better," Google blog, February 23, 2024.

3   Will Douglas Heaven, "Large language models can do jaw-dropping things. But nobody knows exactly why," *MIT*

Technology Review, March 4, 2024.

4 Charles Kaiser, "March on Washington: the day MLK – and Dylan and Baez – made hope and history rhyme," the *Guardian,* August 28, 2023.

5 Matt Growcoot, "AI Image of Tiananmen Square's Tank Man Rises to the Top of Google Search," *PetaPixel,* September 27, 2023.

6 Kevin Sullivan and Lori Rozsa, "DeSantis doubles down on claim that some Blacks benefited from slavery," the *Washington Post,* July 22, 2023.

7 David Halberstam, *The Powers that Be* (Champaign University of Illinois Press, 2000).

8 "The Faces of the American Dead in Vietnam: One Week's Toll," June 27, 1969.

9 100,000 Faces (now 535,000 due to more deaths from COVID), https:// mkorostoff.github.io/ hundred-thousand-faces/.

10 "Faces of Auschwitz," https:// facesofauschwitz.com.

11 Seth Mydans, "Cambodians Demand Apology for Khmer Rouge Images With Smiling Faces," the *New York Times,* April 13, 2021.

12 *Ibid.*

13 Amber Terranova, "How AI Imagery is Shaking Photojournalism," *Blind* magazine, April 26, 2023.

14 *Ibid.*

15 @michaelchristopherbrown, "THIS IMAGERY IS NOT REAL," Instagram, April 4, 2023.

16 Luke Taylor, "Amnesty International criticized for using AI-generated images," the *Guardian,* May 2, 2023.

17 *Ibid.*

18 Naama Riba, "These Holocaust AI Generated Images Distort History," *Haaretz,* February 1, 2023.

19 *Ibid.*

20 "Exhibit A-i: The Refugee Account," https//www.ehibitai.com.au.

21 Hilary Whiteman, "These images aren't real, but for some refugees they depict a painful truth," CNN, June 26, 2023.

22 Will Douglas Heaven, "Generative AI can turn your most precious memories into photos that never existed," *MIT Technology Review,* April 10, 2024.

23 https://www.yurenev.com/ silent-hero-intro

CHAPTER FOUR

1 Umberto Eco, *Travels in Hyperreality: Essays* (New York: Harcourt Brace Jovanovich, 1986).

2 Press Association, "Alan Kurdi image appeared on 20m screens in just 12 hours," the *Guardian,* December 15, 2015.

3 *Ibid.*

4 Brandon Griggs, "Photographer describes 'scream' of migrant boy's 'silent body,'" CNN, September 3, 2015.

5 Peter Bouckaert, "Dispatches: Why I Shared a Horrific Photo of a Drowned Syrian Child," Human Rights Watch, September 2, 2015.

6 Jon Henley, Harriet Grant, Jessica Elgot, Karen McVeigh and Lisa O'Carroll, "Britons rally to help people fleeing war and terror in the Middle East," the *Guardian,* September 3, 2015.

7 *Ibid.*

8 Paul Slovic, Daniel Västfjäll, Arvid Erlandsson and Robin Gregory, "Iconic photographs and the ebb and flow of empathic response to humanitarian disasters," PNAS, January 10, 2017.

9 Charlie Warzel, "The Great Social Media – News Collapse," *The Atlantic,* November 3, 2023.

10 David Bauder and the Associated Press, "America has lost one-third of its newspapers and two-thirds of its newspaper journalists since 2005 despite widespread outcry, study finds," *Fortune,* November 16, 2023.

11 Jacob Liedke and Luxuan Wang, News Platform Fact Sheet, Pew Research Center, November 15, 2023.

12 David Bauder, "Study shows 'striking' number who believe news misinforms," AP News, February 15, 2023.

13 Naomi Forman-Katz, "Americans are following the news less closely than they used to," Pew Research Center, October 24, 2023.

14 Hannah Arendt, *The Origins of Totalitarianism* (New York: Schocken Books, 1951).

15 Marianna Spring, "Omer and Omar: How two 4-year-olds were killed and social media denied it," BBC, October 25, 2023; see also Fred Ritchin, "Regarding the Pain of Others in Israel and Gaza: How Do We Trust What We See?" *Vanity Fair,* November 2, 2023.

16 "100 Photographs: Soweto Uprising" (video), Aryn Baker/ Soweto and TIME staff, "This Photo Galvanized the World Against Apartheid. Here's the Story Behind It," *TIME,* June 15, 2016.

17 Mike Ahlers, "Nixon's doubts over 'Napalm girl' photo," CNN, February 28, 2002.

18 *Ibid.*

19 Nancy K. Miller, "The Girl in the Photograph: The Vietnam War and the Making of National Memory," *JAC,* 2004.

20 Gina Martinez, "TIME Photographer James Nachtwey Presented the 'Napalm Girl' With a German Peace Award. Read His Speech," *TIME,* February 13, 2019.

21 Michael E. Ruane, "A grisly photo of a Saigon execution 50 years ago shocked the world and helped end the war," the *Washington Post,* February 1, 2018.

22 Fred Ritchin, "The March of Images," the *New York Times,* June 10, 1991.

23 Fred Ritchin, "Syrian Torture Archive: When Photographs of Atrocities Don't Shock," *TIME,* January 28, 2014.

24 @samarabuelouf, Instagram, October 14, 2023.

25 @samarabuelouf, Instagram, December 20, 2023.
26 Vaibhav Vats, "India's Hindu Extremists Are Trolling the Israel Conflict," *The Atlantic,* October 26, 2023.
27 Content Authenticity Initiative, contentauthenticity.org.
28 Tiffany Hsu, *ibid.*
29 Tiffany Hsu, *ibid.*
30 Michael Segalov, "Don McCullin: 'Photographing landscapes takes my mind off all I've seen It's healing," the *Guardian,* September 16, 2023.
31 Ben Cosgrove, "W. Eugene Smith's Landmark Photo Essay, 'Nurse Midwife,'" *TIME,* July 21, 2013.
32 *Life* magazine, December 24, 1951.
33 Vicki Goldberg, *The Power of Photography* (New York: Abbeville Press, 1991).
34 John McArthur and Krista Rasmussen, "How successful were the millennium development goals?" the *Guardian,* March 30, 2017.
35 Marie Monique-Robin, *The Photos of the Century* (Cologne: Evergreen/Taschen, 1999).
36 Fred Ritchin, "Columbine Students Are Asking: Will Sharing Photos of the Dead Change Our History of Violence?" *TIME,* April 18, 2019.
37 Neil Postman, *Amusing Ourselves to Death: Public Discourse in the Age of Show Business* (New York: Viking Penguin, 1985).
38 Nelba Márquez-Greene, "Stop Asking Those Closest to Tragedy to Do the Heaviest Lifting," the *New York Times,* July 1, 2022.
39 Issa Touma, *Women We Have Not Lost Yet* (Marseille: André Frère Editions, co-edition with Paradox, 2016).

CHAPTER FIVE
1 Fred Ritchin, "What is Magnum?" *In Our Time: The World As Seen by Magnum Photographers* (New York: W.W. Norton, 1989).
2 Jason Farago, "When Everyone Becomes a War Photographer," the *New York Times,* October 12, 2023.
3 Ritchin, *ibid.*
4 Philip Jones Griffiths, *Vietnam Inc.* (New York: Collier Books, 1971).
5 Fred Ritchin, "The Photography of Conflict," *Aperture,* Winter 1984.
6 https://archive.nytimes.com/www.nytimes.com/specials/bosnia/index.html
7 Rasmus Bellmer and Frank Möller, *Peace, Complexity, Visuality: Ambiguities in Peace and Conflict* (London: Palgrave Macmillan, 2023).
8 Darcy DiNucci, *Print,* November/December 1996.
9 Jim Goldberg, *Rich and Poor* (New York: Random House, 1985).
10 https://nosestanmarcando.com.
11 https://thewhalehunt.org.
12 Pesala Bandara, "Meta's AI System Can Replicate Images in Your Brain in Milliseconds," October 25, 2023.
13 https://bjoernkarmann.dk/project/paragraphica.
14 Henri Cartier-Bresson, *The Decisive Moment* (New York: Simon & Schuster, 1952).
15 Rebecca Carballo, "Using A.I. to Talk to the Dead," December 11, 2023.
16 Kevin Kelly, "Gossip is Philosophy," *Wired,* May 1, 1995.
17 John Berger, "Uses of Photography," in *About Looking* (New York: Pantheon Books, 1980).
18 Shimrit Ben-Yair, "Magic Editor in Google Photos: New AI editing features for reimagining your photos", Google blog, May 10, 2023.
19 David Goldman and Matt Sedensky, "Lives Lost: At veterans' home, towering legacies of the dead," AP News, May 22, 2020.
20 James Reynolds, "Last Suppers," https://www.james-reynolds.com/last-suppers.
21 Clara Jeffery and Emilie Raguso, photo essay by Celia A. Shapiro, "Last Suppers," *Mother Jones,* January 2004.
22 Laura Stampler, "These Are the Last Meals of Innocent Men Who Were Executed," *Business Insider,* February 21, 2013.
23 Susan Sontag, *On Photography* (New York: Farrar, Straus and Giroux, 1977).
24 Robert Sackett, "Pictures of Atrocity: Public Discussions of *Der gelbe Stern* in Early 1960s West Germany," *German History,* Volume 24, Issue 4, October 2006.
25 John Berger and Jean Mohr, "Appearances," *Another Way of Telling* (New York: Pantheon Books, 1982).
26 John Berger, *About Looking* (New York: Pantheon Books, 1980).
27 Elie Wiesel, "The Trivializing of the Holocaust," the *New York Times,* April 16, 1978.
28 Agata Pyzik, "Painting the unpaintable: Gerhard Richter's most divisive work returns to Auschwitz," the *Guardian,* March 5, 2024.
29 Fred Ritchin, "The Eternal Present and the Contested Past," in Anton Kusters, *1078 Blue Skies/4432 Days* (Heidelberg: Kehrer Verlag, 2021).
30 *Ibid.*
31 Mark O'Connell, "Why You Should Read W. G. Sebald," *The New Yorker,* December 14, 2011.
32 Rick Poyner, "W. G. Sebald: Writing with Pictures," *Design Observer,* December 21, 2010.
33 W. G. Sebald, *The Rings of Saturn* (London: New Directions Books, 1998).
34 Elie Wiesel, *Night* (New York: Hill & Wang, 1960).
35 Andy Grundberg, "Photography View: Stieglitz Felt the Pull of Two Cultures," the *New York Times,* February 13, 1983.
36 Mark Pesce, "The Last Days of Reality," *Meanjin,* Summer 2017.
37 Ron Suskind, "Faith, Certainty and the Presidency of George W. Bush, the *New York Times Magazine,* October 17, 2004.

38 Michael Kimmelman, "How the World Closed Its Eyes to Syria's Horror," the *New York Times*, December 14, 2016.
39 Charles Simic, "Expendable America," *The New York Review of Books*, November 19, 2016.

CHAPTER SIX
1 Melissa Heikkilä, "How do you solve a problem like out-of-control AI?" *MIT Technology Review*, May 16, 2023.
2 Will Oremus and Pranshu Verma, "These look like prizewinning photos. They're AI fakes," the *Washington Post*, November 23, 2023.
3 "How it works," Content Authenticity Initiative, https://contentauthenticity.org/how-it-works.
4 News Platform Fact Sheet, Pew Research Center, November 15, 2023.
5 See, for example, Sophie J. Nightingale and Hany Farid, "AI-synthesized faces are indistinguishable from real faces and more trustworthy," PNAS, February 14, 2022.
6 Hema Budaraju, "New ways to get inspired with generative AI in Search," Google blog, October 12, 2023.
7 Thor Benson, "This Disinformation Is Just For You," *Wired*, August 1, 2023.
8 María Luisa Paúl, "Students made a racist deepfake of a principal. It left parents in fear," *The Washington Post*, March 14, 2023.
9 Emanuel Maiberg, "IRL Deepfakes," 404 Media, March 28, 2024.
10 Nadeem Badshah, "Nearly 4,000 celebrities found to be victims of deepfake pornography," the *Guardian*, March 21, 2024.
11 *Ibid.*
12 Guy Hedgecoe, "AI-generated naked child images shock Spanish town of Almendralejo," BBC, September 23, 2023.
13 Teresa Hulzar, "Child sex abuse content is exploding online. We're losing the fight against it," *USA Today*, March 11, 2023.
14 Katie McQue, "Child sexual abuse content growing online with AI-made images, report says," the *Guardian*, April 16, 2024.
15 John Pizzuro, "AI is coming for our kids – we need Congress to act," *The Hill*, September 25, 2023.
16 Marika Tiggemann, "This image has been digitally altered,' disclaimer labels are meant to protect viewers' body image, but do they work?" *The Conversation*, November 21, 2021.
17 Natasha Tiku, Kevin Schaul and Szu Yu Chen, "These fake images reveal how AI amplifies our worst stereotypes," the *Washington Post*, November 1, 2023.
18 Luba Kassova, "Where are all the 'godmothers' of AI? Women's voices are not being heard," the *Guardian*, November 25, 2023.
19 Zoe Williams, "In a dark world, a light is held by those who make it harder for the powerful to lie," the *Guardian*, January 1, 2024.
20 Michael Beschloss, "The Ad That Helped Reagan Sell Good Times to an Uncertain Nation," the *New York Times*, May 7, 2016.
21 It was meant to be a three-day assignment, but on the second day the President was wounded in an assassination attempt by John Hinckley Jr.
22 John Szarkowski, Introductory essay, *Mirrors and Windows: American Photography since 1960* (New York: The Museum of Modern Art, 1978).
23 Helen Coster, "Fewer people trust traditional media, more turn to TikTok for news, report says," Reuters.com, June 13, 2023.
24 https://wwlight.org.
25 Burrow-Giles Lithographic Company v. Sarony, 111 U.S. 53 (1884), JUSTIA U.S. Supreme Court website.
26 "C2PA in DALL·E 3," OpenAI blog.
27 https://fourcornersproject.org.
28 "Time & Life," Time.com, December 31, 2000.

CHAPTER SEVEN
1 See Kenan Malik, "We think loneliness is in our heads, but its source lies in the ruin of civil society," the *Guardian*, March 24, 2024.
2 Richard Stengel, "TIME's Choice of 'You' for Person of the Year in 2006 Was Mocked – But Now Seems Prescient," Time.com, February 28, 2023.
3 *Ibid.*
4 "Robert Capa," International Photography Hall of Fame and Museum website.
5 John Berger, *About Looking* (New York: Pantheon Books, 1980).
6 "Mirrors and Windows: American Photography Since 1960," exhibited July 26–October 2, 1978, Museum of Modern Art, New York.
7 William Blake, "The Marriage of Heaven and Hell," 1790.
8 Jonathan Chadwick and Fiona Jackson, "Dead woman talks to mourners at her own FUNERAL," *Daily Mail* online, August 16, 2022.
9 Amber Louise Bryce, "The rise of 'grief tech': AI is being used to bring the people you love back from the dead," *EuroNews*, December 3, 2023.
10 Faith Karimi, "These six young people died by gun violence. Now their AI-generated voices are sending gun control pleas to lawmakers," CNN.com, February 19, 2024.
11 theshotline.org.
12 Yohann Benchetrit, Hubert Jacob Banville, and Jean-Rémi King, "Toward a real-time decoding of images from brain activity," Meta blog, October 18, 2023.
13 Nita A. Farahany, *The Battle for Your Brain: Defending the Right to Think Freely in the Age of Neurotechnology* (London: Macmillan Publishers, 2023).
14 Paul Virilio, *The Information Bomb* (London: Verso, 2000).

A note on the synthetic imagery

The AI images that were generated for *The Synthetic Eye* were made as part of an inquiry into possibilities, experimenting with what kinds of imagery might emerge that may be useful and even revelatory, as well as those that could be disruptive and distorting. The text prompts are reproduced in whole or in part to give readers a sense of the text-to-image process but are not meant in any sense to be prescriptive. The synthetic imagery created by the author via text prompts was made in collaboration with either OpenAI's DALL·E or Stability AI's DreamStudio between 2022–24.

Acknowledgements

Many have helped make this book, *The Synthetic Eye*, what it is. My wife Carole Naggar, herself a photo historian, was its indispensable first reader. Brian Palmer and Helen Rogan followed as attentive and steadfast editors of the text, enabling the arguments to become more coherent and precise. Bennett Ashley was extraordinarily generous, as he has been before, sharing his legal insights in a rapidly changing environment. Zoe Freilich's help with the preparation of footnotes, captions and imagery has been pivotal to the book's completion. Hanna Hrynkevich also ably assisted with preliminary research, and Shreya Sahai with finishing up.

Sharing resources with colleagues along the way, particularly Marvin Heiferman, Elizabeth Kilroy, Brian Palmer, and Alexey Yurenev, has been essential to the development of the ideas reflected in *The Synthetic Eye*. Thanks as well to many colleagues and friends, among them András Böröcz and Robbin Silverberg, Mark Bussell and Anne Cronin, Debi Cornwall, Maxim and Irina Dondyuk, Melissa Harris, Sue Haven, Kent Klich and Tina Enghoff, Ira Lupu, Susan Meiselas, Mickey H. Osterreicher, Guilietta Palumbo, Robert Pledge, Sylvia Plachy and Elliot Brody, Sarah Putnam, Zahra Rasool, Joseph Rodriguez, Sydney and Christina Spiesel, Larry Towell, Charles Traub, and Pauline Vermare, who illuminated the journey in multiple ways. And a special remembrance of Mark Haven, an extraordinarily empathetic and insightful friend, whose spirit continues to inform. Editors who supported the writing of essays at key moments along the way include David Friend at *Vanity Fair*, Alessia Glaviano at *Vogue*, and Barbara Stauss at *ReVue*. And much gratitude goes to students, former students, and teaching assistants from the International Center of Photography, as well as the Photography and Social Justice Program sponsored by the Magnum Foundation, whose openness to new strategies and ideas has enriched my life in numerous ways.

The many photographers and media-makers who keep on doing the work, inventing new ways to get at complex and pivotal issues, are central to this book, as are the journalists and commentators who keep us aware of the vagaries of an emergent AI. And, of course, the critics who have long reflected on more constructive, ethical uses of the media continue to enlighten many of today's reflections.

My family, Carole Naggar, Ariel Ritchin and Cailey Simmons and Leon, Ezra Ritchin and Emily Rutland, my brother Steve and Andrea, Ruby, Coby and Esther, are at the crucial heart of this endeavor to move things forward, as they always have been.

A special thanks to the good people at Thames & Hudson who believed in and shepherded *The Synthetic Eye* to its completion over the past two years, particularly Andrew Sanigar, Nella Souskova, Ilona de Nemethy Sanigar, Ramon Pez, Sadie Brookes, Lazlo Rugoff, Domniki Papadimitriou and Anabel Navarro.

And a final thanks, tinged with some regret, to all of us, the myriad creators whose work online has been used to train various AI systems without us ever having been, for the most part, consulted.

Be the first to know about our new releases,
exclusive content and author events by visiting
thamesandhudson.com
thamesandhudsonusa.com
thamesandhudson.com.au